Percy Russell

A journey to Lake Taupo and Australian and New Zealand tales and sketches

Percy Russell

A journey to Lake Taupo and Australian and New Zealand tales and sketches

ISBN/EAN: 9783744745697

Printed in Europe, USA, Canada, Australia, Japan

Cover: Foto ©Andreas Hilbeck / pixelio.de

More available books at **www.hansebooks.com**

A JOURNEY TO LAKE TAUPO

AND

Australian and New Zealand

TALES AND SKETCHES.

BY

PERCY RUSSELL,

AUTHOR OF "KING ALFRED," "AFTER THIS LIFE," "THE LITERARY MANUAL,"
ETC., ETC.

LONDON:

E. A. PETHERICK & CO., 33, PATERNOSTER ROW, E.C.

MELBOURNE: 3, ST. JAMES'S STREET.

This Volume

IS

DEDICATED

AFFECTIONATELY TO OUR

RELATIVES

IN

NEW SOUTH WALES AND VICTORIA.

INTRODUCTORY.

THE growth and development of Australia and New Zealand, present the last of the most important and interesting problems that the world can now see solved in respect to the evolution of the nation from the general community. Africa, it is true, is not yet completely colonised, but Africa has its own native races, and it was only in the Austral worlds that there were, a generation or two back, areas entirely unclaimed and vacant, soils geographically removed from the practical politics of Europe, and at first occupied by such small groups that here, if anywhere, the shaping hand of the benign legislator could work unrestrained. It was possible initially to here build up communities of harmoniously co-ordinated classes, whence all evils common to civilised life in

Europe could be wholly eliminated, and here it was possible so to educate and influence the mass of the people that each colony might be legislatively crystallised into a miniature Christendom. The way to this realisation of an ideal, hitherto only dreamed of by Utopian Christian legislators, was clear, and all the usual elements of discord and disorder might easily have been excluded prior to the epoch of responsible government. This last, supplied fully by contingents of God-fearing statesmen, bent on developing a true Christian polity, might, in the issue, have richly crowned a work, glorious as good, and fitly symbolised in the distinctive constellation of the Southern Hemisphere.

It is not for me to say here how the Austral colonies really stand in relation to this ideal polity, but I have ventured, through the medium of an imaginary character, to indicate, at all events, the direction in which much that might have been splendid success has been marred by incompleteness and even failure.

In case some should consider me singular and eccentric in these views, I will here cite writers personally unknown to me, but whose plain, outspoken books have greatly impressed my mind in respect to the existing state of society in Australasia.

In "New Zealand of To-day," Mr. John Bradshaw

remarks strongly on the purely secular system now enforced in the State schools of the Britain of the South. In 1885 a Bill to compel the reading of the Bible in the State schools was lost by a majority of 32, owing mainly to the opposition of Sir Robert Stout, who was not only Premier, but Minister of Education and President of the Freethought Association of Dunedin. Mr. Bradshaw, however, declares that the large number of votes cast against Bible reading in the State schools does not really represent the true state of feeling in the colony. Many of the colonists side with Mr. Larnach, who holds that the State interfered improperly when it decreed that children should not be taught the elements of religion in the public schools. Mr. J. C. Firth, in his book, "Our Kin Across the Sea," utters a like complaint, and dilates on this advanced infidelity; and Mr. Barlow, in "Kaipara," says: "Freethought has taken strong root in Auckland, and I think the cause is due to the expulsion of the Bible from the New Zealand Government schools."

I am fully aware that over large areas under the Southern Cross a very different state of things prevails, but obviously the immediate outcome of purely secular State schools can hardly be other than a new generation, to whom religion, as understood and felt by their fathers and mothers, is a strange and quite extraneous thing. That Theism, at all events, should be taught through the medium of the schools of the State, is a proposition wherein most men will agree, however widely they may differ among themselves as to doctrine and sect. The difference between an unsectarian Theism and secularism is wide indeed, and—let doctrinaires allege what they may—the end of the latter is intermittent anarchy and social confusion. True religion is undoubtedly the foundation of society, and when *that* is seriously disturbed, nothing remains fixed or stable. As Chalmers says, Infidelity gives nothing in return for what it takes away, and, after all, without God or religion to what end do men and women labour and live?

In conclusion I must express my sincere thanks to the Proprietors of the *European Mail* and the *Hull News* for permission to reproduce "The Treasure Tree," which originally appeared in those journals.

TRENT HOUSE, TRENT ROAD,
    BRIXTON HILL, S.W.
       1889.

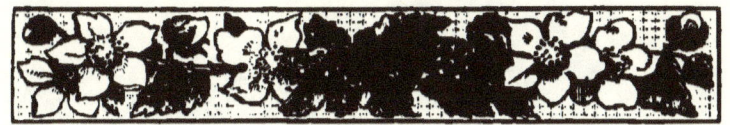

CONTENTS.

Tales.

	PAGE
A Journey to Lake Taupo	1
An Austral Theocracy	43
The Treasure Tree	57
A Mad Passion	113

Sketches.

Edward Gibbon Wakefield	161
Tasmania: a Sketch and a Prophecy	173
Victoria and England: a Contrast	181
Australian Art	191
United Empire	207
A Melbourne Tragedy	213

THE BIRTH OF AUSTRALIA.

Not 'mid the thunder of the battle guns,
Not on the red field of an Empire's wrath,
Rose to a nation Australasia's sons,
Who tread to greatness Industry's pure path!
Behold a people thro' whose annals runs
No damning stain of falsehood, force or fraud,
Whose sceptre is the plough-share—not the sword—
Whose glory lives in harvest-ripening suns.
Where, 'mid the records of old Rome or Greece,
Glows such a tale? Thou canst not answer, Time!
Her shield unsullied by a single crime,
Her wealth of gold, and still more golden fleece,
Forth stands Australia, in her birth sublime—
The only nation from the womb of Peace!

TALES.

A JOURNEY TO LAKE TAUPO;

OR,

THE LIFE AND OPINIONS OF THOMAS MOYLE.

I.—THE START FOR LAKE TAUPO.

THE most northern of the three islands designated New Zealand simply, includes in the source, basin, and valley of the Waikato River some of the most beautiful scenery in the southern hemisphere. Here Mount Ruapehu soars up over 9,000 feet, far into the regions of perpetual snow; here, too, is the frequently thundering and terrible Tongariro and the famous Lake Taupo, which stretches a sea-like expanse of some 30 by 20 miles, and is linked to much curious and highly poetic Maori legend; while in this region we have the central thermal springs and natural sanatorium of the north island, to say nothing of the beautiful and matchless pink terraces which were overwhelmed by the awful convulsion of June 10, 1886, when from the south-western portion of the grand Tarawera mountains there burst forth the dreadful deluge of fire, stones, and mud which devastated the whole of the surrounding country and quite changed the aspect of nature.

In these regions the mountains are generally clothed with evergreen forests, and here and there the landscape has an indescribable fairy beauty and grace, due to the lovely fern-clad ridges which, seen for the first time by the newly arrived traveller, strike the imagination as something entirely new. Then round Lakes Rotomahana and Rotorua there are a number of great geysers, like those of Iceland, throwing up magnificent columns of boiling water and sometimes filling the whole sky with enormous volumes of steam.

This, or something like it, mingled with sundry grim tales of Maori daring and ferocity in the early days of the colony, was the substance of what my friends told me when I started off on a walking tour to Lake Taupo.

I was young and hopeful—I, John Maclaren—having come out only a few years before to take a clerk's stool in a good mercantile firm in Auckland, and was even anticipating that, in the course of ten or twelve years more I might be earning enough—my salary was slowly progressive—to settle down a married man and become a "somebody" in the place where I had already made many good friends. Moreover, there was a certain young lady "saving up" for me, if nothing untoward occurred, when suddenly misfortune came on me in the shape of giddy attacks and a dimness of vision which made neat and accurate ledger work simply impossible. The doctors told me that I wanted fresh air and exercise and entire change, that I ought to leave off working, and that unless

I did so I should probably be invalided for life. I must say this advice was much to my mind. I was a clerk only because I had not seen any other way open to independence, and the lady I was engaged to had set her face dead against an idea of mine to try farming, for which certainly I had neither experience nor skill. Once colonists are settled down, as she and her widowed father were, in a snug competency amid the comforts of "paving and lighting," and in a home which is a replica, with only agreeable variations, of one of old England's middle class establishments, and "roughing" it out in "the bush" seldom recommends itself. There was a reasonable prospect for me in time of getting off the office stool to a comfortable easy chair in the parlour with my two principals, who took a kind and an encouraging interest in me, and I was now rather perplexed and depressed on account of the present than the future.

Well, as I have hinted, my principals came round handsomely, and as business was just then "quiet," suggested that I should try a walking tour to Lake Taupo, and advanced me a quarter's salary to cover expenses and pay cost of lodging at a sort of boarding house they recommended me to try when I had arrived at the great New Zealand sanatorium.

All this was very nice, and I felt exhilarated and restored to a degree that made me feel quite guilty of deception when I wished them good-bye before starting on a tour which was to change and colour the whole course of my existence.

I had very ample directions with me and the names of sundry hospitable settlers who would be ready to give me a night's welcome and comfortable accommodation, and I certainly set out in the best of spirits, while at the bare thought of even temporary emancipation from the ledgers I secretly hated, my eyesight seemed miraculously improved.

I was always a lover of nature and was ever inclined to exclaim, with George Lancaster, the North country poet:—

> It is only a calling for cripples
> To sit in an office and write.

Nothing very special happened to me until I had got quite out into what appeared to me a wilderness, but a wilderness of marvellous beauty and variety. Then I came on some Kauri gum diggers, equipped with their curious spade-handled steel spears for probing about the fallen and buried gum trees; and I fell in with one or two gossipy ne'er-do-wells, who were trying fresh fields and pastures new, to meet, probably, with their usual ill-luck. But it was not until I had been gone over a week that the incident befell me which was the real, and, indeed, the only, cause why this little sketch of my experiences in visiting Lake Taupo came to be written.

I had put up for the evening at the house of a settler —a very intelligent man—originally an agricultural labourer who had emigrated, and who was full of tales of the tough fighting with the natives in Taranaki, when, in the course of our conversation, he enquired how far I meant to go on the morrow. I gave him an idea. He was silent, puffed away at his pipe, and then remarked— "That's a longish pull, and when you've made it I don't think you'll find any place to take you in."

"Oh!" I rejoined, smiling, "I am hardened now, and a bed on the ground is not a killing matter."

"It is a wild bit of country and rough, that you are going through," he went on. "There was a report once of gold being there, but after a small rush it all ended in smoke," and he emphasised the word with a tremendous puff. "Still there is a house somewhere up there, only everybody except the Maoris gives it a wide berth." "Why?" I asked, my curiosity roused. "Well, it is inhabited by a sort of bear in the shape of a man—aye, and a big bear too. He's a character! I caught a sight of him once, and he looked exactly like one of them Druid chaps I once saw in a history of England. The Maoris like him. One or two who have taken to tillage and given up 'long pig' are his neighbours. I believe he speaks their language, but he is generally held to be cracked. When he heard a rumour—it was quite an idle one—of a railway coming down here, he was in a fury and uttered horrible threats as to what he would do if a surveyor came on *his* land. He is an oddity all ways, and one of his peculiarities is a hobby for felling trees. He has built around his house a regular wall of splendid Kauri logs. By the way, they are worth seeing. They are all squared off, like pieces of Portland stone, some six feet long or so, and built up and dovetailed in like masonry. 'If we had a pah like that,' said a Maori to me one day, 'your redcoats would never have got in.'"

My host had more to say about this queer old settler, but I have given the salient points, and when I lay down I must confess I felt an inextinguishable desire to see this strange man and judge for myself; and all that night I had a perfect nightmare wherein Maoris and Druids, mediæval castles and pahs were jumbled up in 'inextricable confusion.

It may well be imagined that when I woke and started on my pilgrimage the next day to Taupo Lake, my thoughts ran much on the strange man of whom I had such an extraordinary account.

II.—Struck Down.

It is always easy to distinguish that magnificent and distinctive New Zealand tree, the sylvan king of the Southern Cross—the Kauri pine—by its dense, dark foliage as well as by its grandeur of stature and the peculiarity that, as it mounts upward, the lower boughs die off and leave the ever ascending tower of timber clear. I was in a rough track winding about some eminences, and now and then opening up splendid views of valley and plain, of grassy plains and close woodlands. Up till now I had been singularly favoured as to weather, and began to calculate on reaching Taupo Lake without encountering even the semblance of a storm. I was already wonderfully restored in health. My eyesight seemed all right again, my head was clear and cool, and I felt again that I was little better than an impostor and ought to be back again in the close, stuffy office at my usual ledger work. "Oh, that I were rich!" I exclaimed that morning, "and that I might ever enjoy all these beauties of nature!" Only I wished most decidedly for a companion, and began to reflect that the lady of my love was much in error in shrinking, as she plainly did, from that close contact with Mother Earth which is the necessary condition of a settler's existence. As I went on I soon became conscious of a strange stillness and, it seemed to me, weight in the air. Occasionally, as I advanced, my view opened out and showed in the distance two or three mountain peaks—one, I fancied, might be Tongariro, but I was by no means certain, and from one of these cloud-capped eminences there streamed forth a singular trail of very thick and sharply-defined smoke, which cut the clear, blue sky in a strange manner for anything so light and naturally soft-looking as smoke. Suddenly I became aware of a rather loud chopping noise, and, being curious to investigate the cause, I went in the direction of the sound and in a few moments saw something through an opening in the undergrowth that quite arrested my steps as well as my eyes.

I looked into a little glade, where, evidently, a number of fine Kauri pines had been felled, for the stumps still remained, and there standing clear and cameo-like against the slanting sunshine as it broke through an opening from the other side, was a man of magnificent proportions —I am myself by no means a pigmy—and with a head like those you see in the sculptured Homers. His beard, snow-white, flowed over his chest for quite a foot or so, and he was now well into the trunk of a fine young Kauri pine, which seemed to quiver beneath the practised strokes of his axe. This, then, was the strange being of whom I had been told. As he now posed before me he was, I thought, less bear-like than leonine, and as he chopped he appeared to be repeating to himself something rhythmical, only nothing exactly articulate reached my ears. The tree was, I saw, about half cut through, and I concluded that he meant to lay it from him, when without the slightest warning, there was a loud concussion in the air, a wind—I never experienced anything so appallingly abrupt—smote the top of the pine, which rose above most of the others and, to my unspeakable horror. I saw it literally spin rapidly round on the butt whence it was so nearly severed, and then, ah, then! it came down with a shock like thunder, and for a moment I saw nothing!

I am not, happily, deficient either in nerve or presence of mind, and I made but a leap or two and eagerly looked to see what had become of this strange woodman. At first, with a thrill of thankfulness, I fancied that he had entirely escaped, but the next moment I perceived that he was entangled in the head of the tree and pinned down by one of the branches. Fortunately, my strength had quite returned, but before I could release the prostrate man, who uttered not a sound, I was obliged to find the axe and do the hardest bit of chopping that I ever did in all my life. Then, and only then, did the sufferer open his eyes and reward me with a grateful look. It was now evident that he must be seriously hurt, although no blood was to be seen anywhere, and his head and face had escaped perfectly unscathed.

I had of late been a constant and, I believe, an apt pupil at some ambulance lectures, and was fully able to give first aid to the injured. The obvious difficulty, however, was how to move so bulky and heavy a man, and the more so as I feared for internal injuries and fancied that not a few bones had yielded to the fearful shock. Presently he still further revived, thanked me with a mild and very collected voice, and drew my attention to what he had noticed and I had not, namely, the fact that the sky was now overcast with an ominous gloom, while the upper branches of the trees were whipping about in a tremendous wind.

"My house is there"—he pointed to an opening in the glade. "It is quite close. If you will go for me you'll find a Maori inside—a woman—that does not matter—she is strong and you can get something to carry me home on. I shall never walk again, I fear. And the trees will henceforth be safe from me," he added, with a smile which made his face, large as it was, look very childlike and simple.

I lost no time, it may be readily imagined. The house was easily found, standing within its strange and cyclopean walls of hewn timber, and I presently hurried back with a hastily improvised litter and the Maori woman in charge—a fine, stalwart specimen of her race, but already on the somewhat haggard middle age period of what had once been considerable personal attractions. I wasted no time in useless questions, and in a few minutes we were on our way back, carrying our heavy burden as carefully as possible, and just as we got inside the house, the storm, of which fitful gusts had warned us, broke in appalling fury overhead and a blaze of blinding lightning filled the whole place.

I am not, as will presently appear, writing a mere

sensational story, romance or novel, but a history of a very strange man and a still stranger life—a bit of real human drama—that, but for the accident of my walking tour to Taupo Lake would never have been known perhaps, and, therefore, I shall not linger over artistically devised interludes, or dressing up for startling situations, but pass on rapidly to give simply what is salient and essential to enable the reader to comprehend what is to come, only premising that that something is well worthy of thoughtful attention.

All idea of proceeding to Lake Taupo was for the present abandoned by me, as the injured man expressed a strong desire that I should remain with him. He had evidently taken what is popularly called " a great fancy" to me, and I soon found him to be both original and eccentric. He told me that no doubt I had heard of his " bad character " and "misanthropy." " But the truth is," he went on, " I have preferred much to be alone here. I have found in the productions of the natural world around me in this place an ample fund of material to employ myself. Moa, the Maori woman, does all the domesticities needed, and, until this totally unexpected calamity, I have been living free and contemplative, and utterly oblivious of the date of the year or even the month, and very often of the name of the day itself." It struck me, very soon after my introduction to the proprietor of this strange house in the wilderness, that there must be something unusual about him, and every hour I spent with him confirmed the impression more and more.

The effects of the deplorable accident that had attended our first introduction to each other, rendered him greatly dependent on aid, and he frankly confessed that I pleased him much as a nurse. He told me that he had, in the pride of his physical strength, never contemplated what he called his humiliating defeat, and at last one day he said plainly, that if I would consent to stay with him I should be well rewarded. "It won't be for very long," he remarked dreamily. "I know better than any doctor what will be the effects of this accident, and if you like to make up your mind to throw in your lot here, I can, I think, make it worth your while." He saw I hesitated—as, indeed, was only natural, I think, at such a startling proposal—and then he went on, "This accident has been a sort of judgment on me for my self-sufficiency. I thought I had ordered all things so well as to be absolutely self-contained and self-supporting, and dreaded nothing but the coming of a railway"—and, wrecked and impotent as he now was, he laughed aloud—"but I have been rebuked by a gust of wind and a slip of an axe, which tool I thought I had perfected. Do you know I have got Moa, the Maori woman here, to spread her fingers out on a log, and have struck fair and straight between more quickly than you could count them! Ahem! That's all over now. But I dread your going, my boy. You mustn't do your good by halves. If you stay by me till the end, I'll adopt you as the old Romans did sometimes, and you won't find the heirship half a bad thing." He was silent a moment, while I fear I looked on him with anything but a properly grateful expression of face, and then muttered half to himself, "I have done a good many eccentric things in my time, why not one more?"

III.—A House in the Wilderness.

It was not long before I somehow settled down into what was to me a very novel form of existence. I was astonished at myself for yielding to the solicitations of my singular host, and still more astonished at the readiness wherewith I fell into the ways and routine of nursing. Something to me, at least, was very fascinating about this old man. He was a crippled giant to my imagination, and his venerable beard and large, bold features reminded me of a sculptured Moses that had much taken my youthful fancy.

Much has been finely written in novels about love between the sexes, but I think no adequate pains have been taken to paint the development of friendship. At all events, I know not how or why, a strong friendship sprung up within me towards this lonely old man, and although with each day I knew well that I ought to be up and off, I had really no power, or inclination it may be supposed, to stir, and settled down to the routine of quite a new life to me with an apathetic contentment that was born of the powerful but subtle fascination this old man exercised over all within his immediate influence.

The house, castle-like in its solidity, was quite surrounded by a high wall of squared and masonry-like Kauri logs, and inside there was a quaint old-world look about the arrangements which struck me, colonial bred, as remarkable. The old man had one room specially his own, filled with old books, many folios strange to me, ancient carved furniture, such as is rarely to be seen in the Austral world; and in his conversation he often fell into disquisitions on subjects quite new to me, and in which I could hardly follow what certainly seemed at the time rather rambling discourses.

The more I knew of Thomas Moyle, for that was the name of this singular recluse, the more he interested and, at the same time, surprised me. Except for the crippling consequence of his late misfortune, which had deprived him of the use of his legs, he now seemed little the worse, and he delighted, I could see it plainly, more and more in my society. He had a raised bed made under a window in one of the rooms, so as to enable him to look out on a little shrubbery or plantation he had formed within his walls of Kauri pine. Here grew an abundance of the luxuriant Tara ferns, with their edible roots, and a fine vine climbed about and over the verandah. Some English flowers had been planted here, which gave colour to what was a beautiful shady retreat, filled with a tremulous green light, except when the noon sun poured directly down. Moyle had been, he told me, an enthusiastic gardener, and was fond of repeating that a garden, which he called "an Eden to the wise," had always been the inclination of kings and the choice of philosophers, for, as he added, when Epicurus taught that pleasure was the chiefest good, " he in a garden's shade the sovereign pleasure sought."

Day by day I discovered in Moyle some new and amiable trait, and it was to me a marvel how such a man could have been thus buried in the utter obscurity of this wild retreat.

Little by little Moyle had elicited from me the simple facts and circumstances of my commonplace and uneventful life, and one day he asked me abruptly why I did not send for Miss Mercer (that was the name of the young lady I considered myself engaged to) and marry her!

He saw my look of astonishment and smiled. "I suppose she would not consent if we asked her," he remarked. "It is but one more instance of the fact that we are, all of us, enslaved by a thousand artificial restraints on our personal freedom. If we were but free, we might, perhaps, be happy. I came myself into this wilderness in search of liberty, and this bed on which I am now lying shows how I have fared in that direction." He had began lightly, but he ended with evident emotion, and we were both silent. Presently he went on: "It is selfish of me, I know, to keep you here. I ought to be altruistic—you know the cult, I dare say, of the Positivist idiots—and endow you with everything I have, and send you on your way rejoicing. Well, well, my boy, wait a while. But if you like to marry, and the lady will consent, why, have her here as soon as possible. I would the house had some youth and beauty in it. I dare say the lady is young and pretty, eh?"

What could one say to speech like this? Moyle amazed me more and more, and yet withal I had an instinctive feeling that he held something in reserve, which I began to long and yet still dreaded to know.

What more perplexed me, perhaps, was the fascination this helpless old man exercised over me. All along I had felt that I ought to pass on and go my way, but I was utterly impotent to put the resolution into execution. He seemed to hold me to his side by a kind of spell, which I could not in the least resist. He had, in a manner, taken possession of me and appropriated me, as it were, for his own. My friends at considerable trouble and some expense, sent me urgent remonstrances to return, and Miss Mercer herself wrote a letter, which I considered exceedingly unkind and stupidly sarcastic, wherein she remarked that no doubt I found the Maori charms of Mr. Moyle's establishment too great an attraction to leave me any inclination for going back to humdrum business and civilised recreations, and more in the same strain, and yet all the time I knew well that if the writers had only come under the personal influence of this strange old man, under the same circumstances as I had, they would most likely have stayed with him as I was doing then.

There was such a depth of genuine and sympathetic feeling in Moyle's warm, brown eyes, such a tenderness in the gentle curve of his full-lipped mouth, so far as it could be seen amid the bush of his venerable beard!

IV.—An Adopted Son.

How rapidly one's ideas alter sometimes with changed circumstances. Something, I know not what, seemed to draw me more to this strange old man, and I resigned all concern in my former life without a pang or regret. I knew well that by my friends and acquaintances I was given up as a lost man—one who had by some wild eccentricity, little short of downright lunacy, suffered himself to be drawn into the service of one who, I found, was held by many to be a mad old settler. I, John Maclaren, who had such excellent prospects, and might in time expect to graduate from clerk to junior partner, had now sunk into the low position of a male nurse and unsalaried attendant to one who, Miss Mercer assured me, in one of her remonstrative letters (for had she not made very careful enquiries?), was commonly held to be a mad old man, who could get no one to consort with him but Maoris as mad and as savage and morose as himself.

Then there was another spell cast over me by Thomas Moyle. As I have confessed, I was, when I went on my fateful walking tour to Lake Taupo, but an ordinary well-informed nineteenth century young man of the middle class, devoted to mercantile pursuits. As we settled down to a sort of daily routine, new developments came. Moyle was a great smoker, and had a large stock of choice tobacco. He delighted in his pipe, and during the afternoon and evening he would discourse to me for hours on all imaginable topics under the sun, interrupted only by the Maori woman, who would bring us in our evening meal. I literally sat at the feet of the old sage, as though he had been another Gamaliel, and I eagerly drank in a flood of information, mostly new and strange to me, respecting the past, present, and sometimes, in a speculative sense, the future of the human race. Now and then some old tattooed Maori would pay us a solemn ceremonial kind of visit, accept with great deference a gift of tobacco, and exchange with the utmost deliberation some sentences in Maori with Moyle. Other visitors we had none.

Although now quite paralysed as to the lower limbs, Moyle was in all respects apparently hale and hearty, and somehow he seemed to gain day by day more and more placidity in his features and to assume quite a different aspect from that he had at first borne at our first strange introduction to each other. He had certainly a venerable aspect; age seemed to rest with a becoming grace upon his somewhat large features, and to my fancy, as I listened to his daily disquisitions, he appeared to bear in his face and brow the signs of a well-spent life. Was I mistaken? Well, we shall see soon enough.

As I have already hinted, this is not exactly a fictitious narrative, and this must be my apology for not "dressing up" the incidents thereof in the approved way of the sensational fiction of the day. In real life some things seem to occur in an isolated manner; some courses of life lead to true no thoroughfares, and in now reproducing the main incidents of the life of Thomas Moyle, I adhere as much as practicable to his own words. The story was told me a bit at a time in the course of our afternoon and evening dialogues, when "work" was over and we blew the "cloud of peace" together. We had quite come to fill the relations of father and son, and it seemed to afford him much satisfaction to explain the present circumstances in which I found him by revealing his singular past history, which he insisted was only due to me if I consented to abandon my own career and take him at his word and cast in my lot with his.

It would be, however, tiresome to give the story as it was told to me in many snatches, and I have therefore, with what little skill I have, thrown the whole together in a connected form.

V.—THE LIFE OF A WOULD-BE REFORMER.

THERE can be no doubt that I was a strange child. At eight I was caught saying that something had happened "when I was young," and two years later I startled my mother—a dear, good-souled, but perfectly matter-of-fact, unimaginative woman—by asking her if she had ever thought that "all things ended badly?"

I had ready a string of miserable illustrations from history, such as the ruins of all the ancient empires, &c., but I had no opportunity for displaying this part of my precocity, as I well remember that my father, who had overheard me, boxed my ears and told me that I should end badly myself if I didn't amend my ways. My parents, plain working people, were neither happy in me nor I in them, but—we lived in quite a rustic Bedfordshire village—the vicar took much notice of me, and one of his daughters gave me special care in the Sunday school. I picked up, one way and the other, a desultory sort of education, all odds and ends thus jumbled up together, but as I grew older I took a violent dislike to work in a manual sense, and to tools, which will surprise you, seeing how you found me chopping down trees. Ah, me, just one too many!

I displayed, all at once, great aptitude for drawing, and somehow the vicar and his daughter, my Sunday school mistress, persuaded an architect and surveyor in the neighbourhood to take me as a sort of apprentice, pupil, clerk and I know not what, giving me board and lodging but no salary. My father and mother both died soon after, leaving but a trifle for me, and I was quite alone in the world. Although born of and really one of the people, as I now admit, I was very different then, and much of my youthful ambition lay in the clothes-horse direction so scathingly satirised by Carlyle, and I looked forward to being well dressed and becoming engaged to some young lady—emphatically such—and there my ambition at that time ended. I did not gaze so far as marriage. Well, I am confessing everything; and after all, I dare say I was not so very different then from the majority of young fellows of my age.

By this time I had grown skilful as a draughtsman but a friend suggested that I might add to my income, which was at this period very small, by "doing an article" for the local paper; and as I had always been, on the whole, a studious and reading youth, I had taught myself, as I then thought, the art of composition out of some grammar that dealt with the subject rather fully. I tried my hand. My early attempts were poor things enough, but they somehow got into print, and from one thing to another, I fell at last into a course of journalism. I removed to Exeter, where an opening on a rather good paper presented itself, and, laying aside the office work of my old master, I soon found myself a member of the Fourth Estate.

Thus far I had not done badly, and as my rise was mainly due to my own exertions, as I fondly fancied, and my inborn ability, I ought to have continued in the same course. My idle desire to be "the human clothes-horse" satirised by Carlyle had long ago departed, and I was really settling down into a steady, industrious course, which should have at last conducted me to an honourable independency, when I had the misfortune, or, let me say at once, the misery—well, I cannot find a fitter phrase than the threadbare and hackneyed one—to fall in love. The object of my new passion, which changed my whole destiny and has landed me here and chained you to the side of a crippled, baffled, and, in some things, as you will see, foolish old man, was the second daughter of an Exeter physician, a very proud, reserved, austere man, who lived beyond his means and regarded "newspaper men" as entirely beneath his social notice.

I am not writing a novel, but simply telling a story, and one, I admit, with a purpose, so I pass over all that is irrelevant to the main issues of my confessions.

We were married, and, much against the advice of her relatives and friends, Lily Stanton became my wife.

We were then most decidedly in love. I had obtained a month's vacation, and for that brief period life to us was Elysian. Lily was fond of quiet, restful, contemplative and refined enjoyments, and as she was then to me my all in all, everything went well. But, alas! here again my childish touch of philosophy that everything ends badly was soon realised. I went back to work, and stimulated by a new-born ambition, applied for and obtained a post in London, where I was to be both editor and sub-editor, and, in consideration of getting up a whole paper, to receive what seemed to me a very large salary. This was the beginning of all my misfortunes, but at first everything seemed very bright indeed.

At that time I was young, ardent and impulsive. I verily believe that on returning from the honeymoon my real affection for Lily was much increased, but I suppose there is a strong strain of the practical in my nature, and I said to myself, "Now is the time for work, now is the time to achieve something." I was intellectually ambitious, and had even then worked out the path I fondly fancied would lead at once to distinction and to well-doing in a truly philanthropic aspect. I was entirely dissatisfied with all existing systems of governments and with the accepted principles and canons of political economy; especially was I dissatisfied with such, to me, horrible things as competition and the survival of the fittest.

I employed all my thoughts and my leisure, which latter was exceedingly limited, on the subject of social evils of all kinds, and sought to discover why it was that a so-called Christendom was so very unchristian in its practices. I was soon sharply pulled up. An opening occurring, as I fancied, in one of my articles for touching on these topics, I did so, but very slightly and cautiously. The effect was very marked, but not at all in the way I had expected. The proprietors, as it happened, never noticed the change I had made, but some one of those officious, unfeeling, thoughtless persons who never think about consequences to others, wrote direct to my employers, and as a result I was "warned" that a repetition of the offence would be deemed tantamount to my resignation.

This galled me greatly. I was young then and inexperienced, and opposition always made me more resolute in those days to carry out any end I had set before me.

I now systematically studied sociology, and found it in all ways intensely fascinating. I read up all the authorities on both sides, and especially did I study Saint Simon, Louis Blanc, Henry Carey, that enlightened American political economist, who, after all, is the original Henry George, and a host of others. I took copious notes of all that I read, and converted these notes into texts, whereon I began to compose essays; and as I all this time quite faithfully carried out my ordinary duties, it may be readily imagined that I had not any time to myself.

I quite admit that at this time my wife and home, and even our only child, were all completely neglected. I rose early, which my wife resented much, as it woke her "at an unearthly hour," and I was the last in bed, and again made her cross, as I had then had the misfortune to rouse her, as she put it, out of "her beauty sleep." When I returned from the toil whereby we lived I was not, I confess, in a light or recreative mood. All the way home I had been working hard at my social problems, and little passed my lips on arriving, as I was impatient to get to my books and desk, and to resume what I fondly called my *magnum opus*. "Well, Lily, how have you been? Anything new?" was frequently all I said, and yet even now, after the lapse of so many memory-dulling years, I affirm that within I was at that period actually growing fonder and fonder every day of my wife. Unfortunately she was unable, and indeed unwilling, to enter into my plans for the reform of governments, and she even let me know that she considered me extremely foolish to waste my time and strength and deprive myself of all pleasure for what she believed to be a kind of insane dream. I urged on her that she should go about and see things and visit her friends, and when she declared that she had none in London, I advised her to make acquaintance with the neighbours and to interest herself in school and church work.

I believed at this time, in my eggregious folly, that before very long I should be fully recognised as a great social reformer and popular leader, and that, wafted high upon the wave of democratic enthusiasm, we should find our lives revolutionised; that enthusiastic friends would spring up all around us and that henceforth our way would be plain and easy. How I have laughed at myself since! Lily was very different from me. She looked the embodiment of a dream of some fair woman, a poet's ideal outwardly, whereas she was, indeed, what I was not then, practical and full of strong common sense, and, unfortunately for us both, she had a spice of obstinacy. She was one of the best, the kindest and dearest of women. I confess that she sometimes made me feel in secret ashamed, for she, in spite of her refinement and her scrupulous carefulness in attire, would pick up and nurse some poor stray sick animal and make it well again in most cases, with a skill that would have won the admiration of any veterinary surgeon; and she was just as tender and sympathetic to human beings in trouble or distress. Still, she was peculiar in this, that she would rarely associate herself with others, but remained alone and ministered in secret. I did in those dreadful dark days, as they soon became, sometimes feel qualms of conscience, and even wondered whether I was not, after all, only a paltry paper philanthropist, while Lily, who pretended to nothing at all, was really doing something; but then at such times of introspective doubt, I would read over some of my more perfervid declamations on the rights of man and evil of governments as at present constituted, and I soon quieted my mind for the time. My wife had an uncle married, with a large family of grown-up daughters, and in the country one or two other relatives similarly circumstanced. I was always in hopes that she would have some of these young relatives to visit us, but, as may be imagined, they preferred when they did leave home to go to houses where there was something like a population. My wife would not move in this matter, and I dared not do so, because I felt sure that she would wrong me by imagining that I preferred the society of others to hers. It will generally be found that in matters like these, as in others, those who want the least obtain the most. It did gall me sometimes when my wife read out from letters that so-and-so had gone on a visit to such a place instead of coming to us, where they might have wrought such incalculable and enduring good and where a new face would have been as sunshine breaking through the deepest gloom.

Ah! those were terrible and fearful days, and I even now recall them thus faintly with a shudder. Often and often did I meditate casting my great work aside and trying to be as others, but as everybody knows, habits are fearful things to break when once formed, and at this time I seemed to have grown into a sort of habit of solitary work, whence I strove vainly to break away. Lily, too, did not help me. She had now settled down into a kind of permanent disappointment plainly expressed in every lineament, but never allowed verbal expression. She was chilling, and oh! so quiet and still that sometimes I would slam the door and throw the chairs about in the room where I worked in a sort of mad revolt, impotent as mad, against the unendurable reproach of this patient, voiceless bearing of one whom I felt in my secret conscience I had used so hardly; and yet all the time, so curious is the working of the human mind, I felt angry too, and considered that Lily was cruelly unsympathetic in not aiding me forward in my great work by continual encouragement!

Well, well, these are painful confessions, and they would not be made did I not deem them due as retributive humiliation on the part of an unhappy man who is constrained to relate all this by an inward uncontrollable prompting to tell all and set everything down without the least bias one way or the other.

But enough for the moment of this. Let me return to facts, which are, after all, the realities of life. I brought my big book into what I fondly thought a pitch of perfection. I cannot now conceive how, with my other practical qualities, I could have been such an idiot as to think for one moment that such a work would be of the least avail; but we are blind to our failings, and I suppose I was full of a foolish pride to see how vast my literary child had grown. I now submitted the work with most pleasurable expectations to a good publisher, and coming as it did from a professional writer, it was well received, and a careful scrutiny promised. For a few days I was in the seventh heaven. I fancied that the volume would be accepted, produced with hot haste, reviewed by all the leading papers, and cited in the House of Commons, and I don't know what besides. Of course all this was very childish and egotistical; but then think what I had done in the way of work. I had really put my very soul and all my domestic enjoyment and happiness that might have been, into this infernal book—for infernal it was soon to prove. Then, too—for I can write coolly of these matters now—there was really a prodigious quantity of thorough painstaking toil in the thing. It was, indeed, a vast library of the whole literature of sociology boiled down and squeezed into one enormous book. I was not long in suspense. The publishers wrote asking me to call. I went eager for, and expectant of, complete triumph. The senior partner of the firm, a mild looking, bald man, wearing spectacles and speaking in a singularly soft voice, received me and said, pointing to my gigantic pile of manuscript on the chair, "Is that really your work?" I assured him most emphatically that it was. "Then," he went on, "I recommend you to burn it and try to forget that you were ever so foolish as to waste valuable time and toil over a book that nobody wants." I was indignant and protested, but he went on, in his even, ambling tone—I think I hear him now: "It is an encyclopædia of Socialism; no one would ever read it without being paid for the job, and it will ruin anybody who tries to publish it so far as it goes. If you have anything new to say, for God's sake, young man, say it in a 32-page pamphlet. I and our reader are amazed that anybody in these days could be such an idiot as to produce a book of the kind; no one wants it. It is really so much waste paper." I was in a towering passion by this time, and declared that he was exceedingly rude, and marched off with my four or five pounds weight of MS. Well, I tried all the publishers, and not one of them would take the work, and most of them added that they would not issue it if paid for doing so. I don't know what demon possessed me, but somehow a species of insane fury fastened on me for a time and I became, to a certain extent, an irresponsible agent.

When I look back now I am amazed that I could ever have been such an idiot as to suppose that the world really wanted such a work. I might as well have striven to popularise a digest of Roman law. For many days I was by turns morose and irritable to the last degree, and without having any *intention* or *animus*, I suppose I spoke to Lily very much like the mixture of bear and tiger that I had unconsciously become. Alas! she did not reflect, and she did not hear or see me when quite alone, or she would never have so foolishly imagined that my splenetic, short, and perhaps, at times, brutal manner, had any reference to *her*. Language, unfortunately, is at times totally inadequate to correct errors of this kind, and moreover we were both of us proud, sullen, and, in truth, sulky, full of cross purposes, and no doubt each cruelly wronging the other. It is indeed curious how completely under certain abnormal conditions those very qualities that *per se* draw individuals to each other, will sometimes set up a violently repulsive action.

To me at this time Lily seemed hard and unsympathetic. Probably to her I seemed the same. I was constantly swayed by violent gusts of passion and she by temper of quite another sort. When I was enveloped, as it were, in a sort of vapour and was blind with my own heat she was quiet, cool and contemptuous. From her lovely lips came the quiet taunting phrase whose lancet-like keenness goes to the quick; from her lovely lips came the measured sentences designed to mortify and wound my self-esteem. When I raved, saying I knew not what, swayed about by the gusts of passion, she would almost whisper the most cutting speeches. Why had I taken her away from her home and all that was dear to her? I did not want a home evidently, why didn't I stay away altogether? I was always wrapped up in foolish dreams, and she might as well be alone! It was vain for me to seek to stem these quiet, almost silent flows of a sort of devastating domestic lava, if I may so term it, which came from her lips. Any attempt at endearments roused her to a fury that was scarcely articulate, and I knew not at times what to do or think. Meanwhile the book remained that had indirectly occasioned all this misery, and I, with a fatal, blind obstinacy resolved to issue it at my own expense! To accomplish this I determined to take more work in, and as this naturally withdrew me more and more from social intercourse, I fear matters went worse still at home. I felt, however, more and more convinced that if only the leading men of the country could be once brought to read my book, which focussed all that needed to be known on sociology, they would no longer hesitate to set about applying the simple and easy reforms that were formulated in the closing chapters! Can you conceive a more absolute infatuation, a more idiotic conceit?

Things were thus, and Lily hardly spoke to me, when I was asked by someone who knew me as a writer if I would go down to Glamorganshire and visit Caldy Isle and explore what are, if I remember aright, called the Bone Caverns of Paviland. A monograph was wanted on the antiquities and remains of the locality, and as the amount offered more than covered the sum required to bring out my precious book, I consented, having hired a substitute to take charge of my London paper during my absence. I hardly liked to tell Lily about this, because I felt guilty at going not for her sake but for that of the book, which was indeed to prove a thing accursed.

Let me hurry on this unhappy narrative. On arriving in Wales I found the work much beyond anything I had anticipated, and on making this known my employer, to my astonishment, generously offered me extra remuneration, "as he wanted the thing thoroughly done, and believed that I could do it well," and moreover agreed, although I had not asked this, to bear the expense of my finding a substitute for my ordinary work on the weekly journal. Surely, I said to myself on receiving this unexpected reply, which contained as earnest money a cheque for £20, I am in fortune's sunshine at last! In truth things began to smile, as I fancied, on me and—for this is more a confession than aught else—I was inwardly conscious that my zeal for the mass of my fellows was not quite so ardent as when my circumstances were worse. I dismissed for the time all care—the first time I had done so for years—and gave myself to the work, which greatly interested me. I had to make very minute examination of the coast, to penetrate into the many dark and dreadful caverns where, even in calm weather outside, the ground swell made great booming waves, and churned up fountains of ghastly spray that seemed to make darkness visible, and I had to interrogate the "oldest" inhabitants to elicit from them whatever of tradition or folk-lore bore on the subject of my researches. I had also to make rough sketches of the relics that came before me, and altogether my work was undoubtedly very engrossing and heavy. I lodged in the house of one of the principal fishermen, and was regarded by him and his family as something very extraordinary indeed.

I began my outdoor task early in the morning, and on returning sat down to my literary work. At first I wrote every other day to Lily, but although I did not mean to do so, I missed writing when the day came round, and on the following I was upset in a boat when exploring one of the old caverns, and had such a soaking that I hastened back and went to bed and never looked even at the post that had come in. It happened that in tumbling out of the boat I gave my head a nasty blow against the rocks, and what with this and a sort of low fever that supervened, I was laid up in a sort of semi-stupid state for some time. When I did get round again I turned at once to the letters and papers that had accumulated, and then—how can I tell it?—learned that our only child had been dead some days!

"I shall not trouble you with any more letters," his mother wrote, "as you do not evidently care what becomes of him or me. If you had stayed at home—where, God knows, I trouble you very little with my company or conversation—this might not have happened, the doctor says. It is now too late. I do not want to trouble you to write. I suppose you will return when it suits your convenience." This awful shock came upon me like a thunder-clap. In my innermost self I had ever been loyal to my wife and child, but now that this catastrophe had come, I seemed to see for the first time how wrong, blind and really selfish I had been. What right, demanded my conscience, had I to sacrifice their present happiness to a problematical future good, and a good which was mainly—I could not honestly deny it—for my own personal glorification? I did not deserve that Lily should thus doubt my affection, but how was she to know that my true self did not correspond with my outward demeanour and my actions? I had felt so convinced within myself of my love for her that I had not hesitated to neglect her utterly, because forsooth at some future time possibly, Fortune might give me the means to do as I liked! I was at first as a man distracted, and the more so when, after reading that dreadful letter from home, I took up another from the proprietors of the weekly paper on which I now mainly depended and read, with eyes that seemed blistered with the few curt lines, that my substitute had been permanently engaged in my place, as he had done the work much better than I, and it was not possible to retain the services of one who dabbled in archæology, and was ready to leave his duties on the slightest excuse!

Truly blow had followed blow with an appalling swiftness and force.

For some time I was veritably stunned. Then I recovered myself a little, and hastily gathering up all my work so far as I had carried it, I rushed homewards with the force of a consuming fire—homewards, I say, where there was now no home to receive me!

The journey was a wild, a fierce excitement; but on approaching the house I dreaded and yet so longed to reach, a strong reaction came upon me. I felt, as it were, the utterly depressing chill of a crowning calamity, and I knocked timidly at my own door—I had no key—and stood on the threshold more like a beggar than the master of the house. I hoped our maid would let me in. I had an unspeakable dread of now meeting Lily, and wished to be in the house first; but no one came, and I knocked louder and more impatiently. Then steps came, the door opened, and Lily stood there with a strange, hard, cruel look in her face, tightly compressed lips, and eyes that blazed with a terrible and deadly light. I stood and stared. A thousand thoughts flashed across my bewildered brain. "Come in," she spoke in a hard, suppressed tone. "You needn't be afraid; the child has been buried, so there is nothing disagreeable in the house!"

"Oh, Lily!" was all I could say, and I walked mechanically in. She looked at me with a contempt that cut me like a whip, but as I staggered into the sitting-room she disappeared, and I was alone. Oh! how I repented during those dark, lonely minutes when I thus regained home, which had no welcome for me, and within which there seemed to my fancy a dreadful atmosphere of death and desolation that blighted all within its fatal influence. With the conviction that Lily was, indeed, entirely estranged, all my early boyish love surged up hot in my veins, all my earlier tenderness revived, and I felt a thousand times fonder than I had ever done of old, and all the agonising time a low, fatal whisper sounded within me that it was now too late. I looked around. All seemed much the same as when I had left that room. The change was in me and her. I rang the bell for the maid, by way of doing something, and judge of my amazement when, in reply to my summons, in walked Lily, with the same hard, fixed look on her face. We looked at each other—she sternly, fiercely even, and I in sadness and sorrow inexpressible to see the change that had come over one once so gentle and timid.

"What did you want?" she asked presently, still with the harsh tone that accorded with her fixed stone-like countenance.

"I? Nothing now."

"What did you ring for?"

"I rang for the servant."

"Then you must want me. There is no other servant here."

"What do you mean?" I asked, amazed at her manner and words.

"What I say. I am the servant here as long as you choose to stay or condescend to keep the house up. You have deprived me of my child, and I must do something or go mad. That is all."

Why did I not yield to the tender, compassionate impulse that came surging up within and fold her to my breast, and so have unlocked the fountains of blessed tears that were welling up, I know, in both of us? But

4

somehow I *could not* then make the first advance. My pride was deeply hurt. I felt keenly the injustice of visiting the death of the child on me, and I turned away muttering I hardly know what.

What ensued during the next few days is far too agonising for me, even at this distance of time, to do more than to outline as to the main facts and hasten on to the crowning catastrophe.

During some days matters went on miserably. Lily practically would not speak to me, and I for my part unhappily wrapped myself up in my wounded pride as in a garment. I quite believe that pride is a most dangerous fault. I felt that Lily was now wrong, for was I not longing to take her to my heart again? It is true I did not exactly admit the truth to myself that unless I humbled myself she could not well know what were my real feelings. I called her unsympathetic, because she evidently believed that the loss of our only child was but a small matter to me. One day she asked me, in a constrained tone, if I did not desire some fitting monument for our little boy's grave. I fear that at the time I looked anything but pleased, for matters were going amiss with me on all sides, and she said no more. Meanwhile, my affairs became bad indeed, and I tacitly acquiesced in our existing domestic arrangements, not at all seeing the way to make both ends meet. Somehow—it was mad obstinacy, I suppose—I grew more doggedly determined than ever to bring out the big book that was to convert the nation to a new theory and practice of political economy. After all, I said to myself, in this temporary madness which descended upon me, a really great book is, as

Luther tells us, a great action. A baby boy—well, we had lost him, and he might have greatly disappointed both of us. A book could be made much more complete, I argued, than a froward child, and I resolved that, come what might, the book should appear. I proceeded cautiously, for I did not want Lily to imagine that the work was not accepted on its own merits; and as she did not, I fancied, know much about such matters, I felt little doubt of keeping the fact of my bearing the expense from her knowledge. Do not imagine that I am not fully conscious now of the enormity of my conduct, but read on and you will see how terribly I was rebuked, and punished too, for my selfishness, conceit and duplicity. One evening I had the whole pile of MS. (and a big thing it was) before me, and also an estimate from the firm who were to produce the work, and as this was a formidable thing, I was making a calculation whether the work might not be reduced to save a sheet in the estimate. It was a chilly autumn evening, and a pretty large fire was burning brightly in the ample grate. I had my back to the door, which had been left ajar, and before me was spread out the large sheet from the publishers of their estimate for printing and binding so many copies of the work. I was so absorbed in the perusal of these figures that I gave quite a start to discover that Lily was behind, and, as I instinctively felt, reading the large document spread out before me.

I knew of her presence, but in a species of moral cowardice which seized me I neither moved nor spoke, and presently she reached over my shoulder, took up the estimate, and said just one word—"Beast!" This was too bad. I sprang up and demanded what she meant. 'You are one," she rejoined; "you grudge your child a monument, and when we are ruined through your folly you actually spend all we possess on a piece of folly which will make you the laughing-stock of everybody! I thought I had married at least a man, but I find I have married a selfish beast, who thinks more of his own rubbishing writings than of his wife or child!" She was evidently in a spasm of passion, and without the least warning of what she was about to do, swept up the precious MS., and, turning round, cast it right on the blazing fire.

I do not know what effect her words might have had on my conscience had it not been for this terrible act. As well almost kill a man as kill a good book, and, anyway, if my book was nothing else, it was a good book. I sprang forward to rescue the precious leaves from the flames, but Lily faced round in a spasm of rage and pushed me off with a strength which was frightful, coming from one so slender and frail. God knows I have never since ceased to grieve over the horrible thing that then happened. In pushing me off with her long outstretched arms, her skirt swept back right in the fire, and I saw, appalled, before she in the least knew what had happened, that she was herself on fire. I shouted out, and tearing the cloth off the table, strove to wrap it round her, but she seemed to have taken leave of her senses and, like a mad creature, burst through the French windows of the room and tore out on to the lawn in front, where the flames roared up far above her head, and formed the most appalling sight I have ever seen.

Let me drop a dark veil over the rest. I was left completely alone. No one blamed me for the accident, but somehow I found those who knew avoided me, and as for strangers, I was certainly in no humour to make any advances to them. In a word, I found my whole life practically destroyed, and then I understood why men often commit suicide. I had no inclination that way, but I then gained an awful experience which has made me much more lenient than I was before to those who find in suicide their only possible resource. It is in itself a stupid thing, however, as Death comes to all; and why, then, take any trouble to do his work? My book had completely perished, and somehow this was a kind of grim consolation. I felt it as a sort of sacrifice, and by so much was I the better. It was in a measure almost like a purging of part of the guilt I felt for the ill way in which I had played the *rôle* of husband and father. Strange irony, when I remember that before marriage I had determined not to be as some, never to think of another woman any more, never to go anywhere without Lily, except strictly in connection with my work, never to gamble or drink, and a host of other excellent things—all these rules I strictly kept. I do not think that I ever broke one, and yet—and yet—such is the horrible irony of circumstance, I had made an end that put the vulgar, drunken, unfaithful husband, so I thought, on quite a pedestal far above me. I had made great professions, too, of affection, and I had imagined myself to be quite a model man! Why, there were bloated wretches I knew on whose shaky knees innocent little girls climbed to kiss lips foul with dissipation and blasphemy, while I, so virgin-like in my acts as well as in my thoughts, was now precipitated into the depths of a very Inferno of slow consuming fire!

I lived quite alone. Some work came to me, and I was by and by regarded as a reserved, taciturn, gloomy man who had wrecked his life in some mysterious way and was never likely to get over it. After a time the old idea of doing good by promulgating a new social cult revived within me, and I began to plague editors with schemes for setting forth my views. I had no longer any notions of a big work, but infinite proposals for articles on the subject. Nothing came of it, but one day a man, who had shown some little interest in me, asked me if I cared to have his advice? I did care, I said, and he then told me that it was quite absurd to suppose that any radical changes like those I had explained to him could ever now be effected in a country like England. What you should do, he urged, is to emigrate to a colony like New Zealand. There a man of ideas like yours might, perhaps, take with the settlers, and there you might get into Parliament and carve out a career for yourself. Worse men than you have gone out as simple colonists and risen to high office. If you don't mind working with your hands first, you can gain the confidence of the mass, and for the rest I should judge a life there is very much better than toiling anonymously, as you and I do, in a dirty London printing office.

It appeared that he was going out and wanted a partner. One part of the world was to me very much the same as another, and we went out in one of the Orient steamers and did very well for some time in a joint affair at Wellington, and saved a little money. He was a single man without any relatives he knew of in the world, and thence his attraction, he said, to me. Unfortunately he died suddenly, having hurt himself somehow in pitching a big drunken Maori out of our house, and at his death, it proved that he had willed all his property to me. Here, however, was another instance of all things ending badly, for I had grown to like him much, and he had, I think, made me a much better man.

Thus came another fit of my old sociological madness. I conceived a grand scheme for making New Zealand the one model country of the world and sought to enter Parliament. I spent much in printing addresses and gave no end of speeches. I had large audiences, and often, to my surprise, then, at the close, all would promise me their votes. Alas! I learned too late that I was being only mocked, and that my orations and Christian economy, as I called it, were simply regarded as a jolly good lark and I was the biggest old idiot in the colony.

Well, well, let me hurry on. The election came and I polled just four votes, and what was infinitely more mortifying, was the way in which I now found myself treated by nearly all with whom I came in contact. Everyone now threw off the mask of hypocrisy that had been worn previously for my express humiliation, and one after another would stop me in the street and say, "Well, Moyle, you mustn't be offended, old man, but we all said you were coming it rather too strong and wanted taking down a peg or two. We know our own business best, bless you, and don't want none of your precious doctrinaires, I think they call 'em, in our Parliament." This was the sum and substance of the sort of cold comfort that was administered to me by men who pretended to be kind friends. As to others I need say nothing. In a word, I found myself successful only in making a kind of political guy of myself; and that is why, in a fit of temper, I cleared out and came down to Lake Taupo and built myself a house in the wilderness and consorted with Maoris, and tried to find peace if not happiness, in communing with nature. Still you will see that, so far as my actual colonising went, things ended badly too, especially when I was fool enough to think I could teach the New Zealanders how to emulate the only one policy that is worthy of reproduction here, that is, the ancient Hebrew theocracy.

Such was the substance of the conversational autobiography which came from the lips of this strange man during a series of evenings which were devoted to the subject and our pipes. Somehow the communication of these singular circumstances of a wasted life seemed to exercise not only a touching but a healing effect on Moyle, and he visibly mended in health, although neither of us had any hope of his ever recovering from his crippled state. He has long since formally adopted me as his son, for he often reminds me of the fact that I am just the age that his boy would have been had he lived, and he has been mainly instrumental in inducing me to take unto myself a wife—not the conventionally-minded lady of my youthful choice, but a well-favoured and comparatively civilised Maori damsel, who always calls him father and promises to make him a happy and proud grandfather in due course.

We all live in much comfort and perfect amity and true Christian accord on this remote clearing, and I at least may well say God be praised for the advice given me to make a walking tour to Lake Taupo, which has led to so much true and, I believe, enduring happiness for others besides myself.

Moyle is, as he says, quite precluded from ever again taking a part in active life; but he particularly desires the true character of his views on the subject of the future government of Australasia to be made known. As he rightly remarks, his long retirement and years of careful reflection on the subject which has always engrossed his thoughts and has lain nearest his heart, have enabled him to fully formulate a policy, and although the electors of Wellington chose, years ago, to make him and his theories a laughing-stock and a jest, he is still desirous to make his true views and moral standpoint known. Under his direction, then, I have drawn up the following account of what he conceives should be the course that ought to be adopted by the colonists. Before, however, giving forth the scheme I have just one word to say, and it is that our manifesto, for such it is, has not been put forth in the expectation of rallying support to me as the representative of Thomas Moyle. Politics lie not in my province. I am "a home-keeping youth" still, my adopted father often tells me, and my wits are too homely for the affairs of State. It were vain for any deputation to wait under our fortress walls of Kauri pine, hewn so true and laid so firmly by him who will never more wield axe; but we think it our joint duty to cast forth the seed, such as it is, of our common ideas. If they fall in stony places they will perish; but it may be that somewhere there are warm hearts eager for the eternal good of human souls, and believing minds who would deem it as far transcending all the vulgar glories of conquering generals or emperor-kings to aid in building up under the Southern Cross the mighty fabric of that Christendom which Europe once dreamed about but has —it is to be feared—abandoned now for ever.

I now give the document which is the true *raison d'etre* of the foregoing confessions.

AN AUSTRAL THEOCRACY.

By THOMAS MOYLE.

———◆———

THE great and conspicuous defect in English governmental policy has always been an absence of *formative ideas for the future.* The notion of planning the lines and organising the conditions on which and through which a people should move onward and upward to a higher development is found only in theory in English statesmanship—never in the practice. Thus it has come about literally that the British Empire, or, as I prefer to call it, the British Dominion, has grown haphazard and by apparent chance, and owes everything to individual rather than to collective and predetermined effort. Many will immediately reply that it is better so, and that England's greatness is due to the free play given to the individual; but surely a policy may be pursued steadily to its appointed goal and not interfere with individual genius, nay, rather should it enlist to its aid the latter, and take care that none of its forces be rendered futile through lack of recognition. All our records, however, teem with melancholy instances of the notorious fact that, although England does not favour formative and definite policies and leaves all her national greatness to be the work of individual efforts, the existing governmental system is such as to neutralise, wherever it comes into contact therewith, the strength of many, who find themselves foiled in the best laid plans for the good of the commonwealth by the utter impossibility of inducing the collective wisdom of the nation to take a comprehensive survey of the future, or to enter into any scheme that would deal with national evils by removing the *causes* thereof, and not simply reducing for a time their effects.

In the case of new lands practically unoccupied, but lying far and wide at the disposal of a sovereign people, amounting to about one person to the square mile, against 477 in the United Kingdom, it might have been hoped that formative statesmanship would have appeared and mastered the situation so as to construct a policy that might be capable of a maximum of good, moral and material, now and hereafter, for the people committed to its charge.

Has it been so? What has actually happened was thus described several years ago in the *Queenslander*:—

"Most Englishmen emigrating from a country in which the framework of civilisation is old and artificial, wherever they settle endeavour, unfortunately, to reproduce that state of society. They fail to see that, in coming to a new land, where nature is so bountiful, and the means of subsistence are procurable with so little labour and in such great abundance from the soil, the pursuits of husbandry should have a preferential claim upon them before all others, and that we should endeavour to reproduce in Australia the merry England of Elizabeth, rather than the anxious, careworn, mammon-worshipping England of Victoria. In view of the fact that the tendency in each of the colonies is towards an augmentation of the non-producing and distributing classes, instead of towards an increase of those which are productive, the outlook for the future is much less satisfactory than we could wish it to be. The population of each of the chief centres of population (including suburbs) in these colonies will serve to show the aggregating tendencies of British colonists in Australia:—Melbourne, having 210,000; Sydney, 140,000; Adelaide, 60,000; Ballarat, 40,000; Sandhurst, 28,000; Brisbane, 27,000; Hobart Town, 20,000; Geelong, 20,000. Here we have over half a million of people, out of a total population of about one million and three-quarters crowded into eight large towns, the biggest of which has confessedly reproduced all the worst features of some of the oldest capitals in Europe—their vilest vices, their filth, their squalor, their crimes, their poverty, and their diseases."

Had invention, however, been beneficially directed to agriculture in the same degree that it has been concentrated on, say, the infernal art of destroying human life, the vocation of the farm labourer generally would have been elevated on a level to that of the town mechanic at the very least, production would have been greatly increased, and the best low-born intelligence of rural districts would not have been compelled, as now, to forsake the country for the town. Feeling so strongly on this point, I have ever regarded with the highest satisfaction the endeavours of those who have sought by their inventive skill to elevate agricultural drudgery to a high and scientific vocation, one to be pursued intelligently by intellectual men fully on a level with the foremost workers in the city manufactory.

Then, too, let us consider how much the evil of concentration and centralisation—the curses of all modern peoples—has intensified since the *Queenslander* wrote, for now we have Melbourne with 380,000, Sydney 332,000, Adelaide 128,000, Brisbane 50,000, Hobart 25,000 (a very moderate increase here), while Ballarat, Sandhurst and Geelong have respectively 41,000, 36,000, and 21,000. We have here considerably over one million of the total population crowded into the purely artificial and more or less injurious influences of urban life.

In things governmental it is obviously easiest to deal with small groups of people, and it is remarkable in sociology that certain special evils of civilisation scarcely exist, and some not at all, outside large centres of population. If it were possible to begin a governmental system with population divided into comparatively small bodies, it would be found that far higher results are to be gained than where immense masses of men are forced together. Man hides man in a sense, and the greater the mass the greater the difficulty of evolving thence a high relative standard of happiness and morality for the majority. To perpetuate on a new continent the social evils and mistakes of England, to unduly encourage by all possible means the concentration of population away from the direct means of subsistence, is surely a bad policy, and one that makes the thoughtful despair of governments altogether as true agencies for bringing on a perfected condition of humanity.

I have said, however, that it is easier to deal with *small* groups of population for all the *formative* purposes of a wise statesmanship, having the future as well as the present steadily in view, and in truth in the *school* we have exactly the conditions that most fully favour the need of the ideal statesman who seeks to evolve from the present a perfected future. Certainly the State can exercise a mighty and, in truth—humanly speaking— an omnipotent power over the people by casting a special matrice of State teaching wherein to mould the minds of the future citizens and give to each the determining bias which, although it may frequently fail in the individual will ever hold good in the mass. How and why is this to be done? it will be asked. The way undoubtedly is to furnish a distinct and truly catholic religious basis for all State school teaching and to let all technics, all physics, all material knowledge follow a deep grounding in religion and its resultant morality. Thomas Carlyle, writing on the subject of government— and he was not what is commonly called a religious man —says: "It seems to me a great truth that human things cannot stand on selfishness, mechanical utilities, economics and law courts; that if there be *not a religious element* in the relations of men, such relations are miserable and *doomed to ruin.*" Let us suppose for a moment, merely by way of argument, that in every State school all instruction rose on the basis of the Bible, that every text-book put into the hands of every boy and girl were written on the assumption that Christianity is a Revealed Religion and that that Revelation is absolutely true; suppose wherever mention has to be made of writers like Herbert Spencer, Huxley, and Darwin, brief notes were given condensing the best refutations of their several assaults on Revealed Religion; and suppose, further, each child were taught that all law, order and discipline, and indeed all that is authoritative in human affairs rested ultimately on the eternal truth of there being not only a Creator of the world and of man, but a daily Upholder, through the agency of an uninterrupted Providence of the universe—suppose all science were subordinated to this idea and children were taught in the mysteries of electricity and of gravitation to recognise but sensible connections between the material universe and its invisible God—can we doubt for one moment that the vast majority of the children thus trained, would grow up better, purer in mind, more industriously disposed, more grateful for the good of this life, more consistently virtuous, and, finally, infinitely happier, as assured, each one of them, of a glorious heritage beyond the grave or the pagan crematorium, which seems just now in such favour with those whose great desire appears to be obliteration.

Observe, in this scheme of mine for State Education I propose no *sectarian* teaching. Let the religion taught as the necessary basis of morality, law, and all obedience to authority, be simply Theism Bible-based, and the main object to educate a people who would be truly democratic, in that they would be theocratic, the only way in which any democracy worthy of the name can ever be permanently established.

The great question seems to me, and none can be more momentous to mankind—is there or is there not a Christendom? If there be one let us build it up into greater strength and a purer type of moral beauty; if there be none, let us make one, and the direct and certain means lie ready to hand in the State schools. Once root out the evil of secularism, and all the rest follows. That I am not at all singular in my views is certain. Mr. Firth, in his admirable book, "Our Kin Across the Sea," points out the terrible spread in the United States of irreverence and downright atheism; and Mr. John Bradshaw, in his equally excellent, but very different, volume, "New Zealand as it is," plainly indicates the enormous injury that New Zealand is sustaining through the banishing of the Bible from the State schools, one of the most deplorable of the very many mistakes that have been made in the government of the Britain of the South.

Education in Australia and New Zealand has reached a crisis, and on the way in which it is morally directed the ultimate destiny of mankind largely depends. For the first time in history since the initial preaching of Christianity there is a sublime opportunity and an ample theatre for the full evolution of a true and permanent Christendom, created and sustained by the great Anglo-Saxon race. But let this opportunity be lost, and let this theatre of the new Austral world be peopled mainly by Agnostics, Positivists and other non-Christian types, and we may well look to see humanity delivered up to that satanic spirit of science which sanctions vivisection and would reduce marriage—a divine and God-ordained institution—to a simple matter of business and physiology—a mere branch of State medicine and of the application of that natural selection and survival of the fittest principle, which is expressly opposed to the teaching of Him who declared that even a sparrow's life was of account in the benign counsels of the Almighty.

Let us see what we may expect from scientists pure and simple. Sir Henry Roscoe, in his inaugural address to the British Association in 1887, actually declared that " Possession fosters content, indolence, and pride. If God should hold in His right hand all truth, and in His left hand the ever active desire to seek truth, though with the condition of perpetual error, I would humbly ask for the contents of the left hand, saying, 'Father, give me this; pure truth is only for Thee.'"

Could a more deplorable example of arrogance be well cited than this? Surely *finality—finality* in moral purity—is what the truly religious man seeks; in other words, freedom from sin. Then comes complete content and peace unspeakable. No devout student of the Holy Scriptures could ever bring himself to utter the bombastic and irreverent nonsense put forth by Sir Henry Roscoe as a sublime enunciation of the scientific spirit of the age, which is for ever carping at the highest of all truth, because it is to the exalted scientific mind tainted with the dogma of *obedience.*

Writing on April 28, 1888, the *Sydney Morning Herald* commenced a leader by asking, " Is England a Christian nation?" The question might well be asked. And then the writer went on to speak of the victory achieved by Mr. Bradlaugh, the arch-atheist, in respect to carrying his Bill for the abolition of oaths. The writer then proceeds to say:—" Up to the passing of this Bill, though most of the old religious tests set by the State had been abandoned, the people not only recognised the existence of a Supreme Being, but were one with the Church by an act of formal acknowledgment, and so one with Christianity. There is left but the individual responsibility and recognition."

It has been said that oaths and tests of a like character open the way to deceit and hypocrisy. Doubtless this may be so, but the evil thereof rests not upon the principle underlying all moral tests, but on the individuals who are guilty of the deceit and the hypocrisy. As well might the murderer complain of the penal law which numbers murder as a crime in the list of offences. Every institution must fence itself about with rules and regulations, and if individuals occasionally overcome these by stratagem, it is only a further argument for their maintenance, as showing what kind of foes are without and trying to enter, in order, when in, to subvert the whole. In truth, if the State were truly Christian there would be but one word on such points, and it is nothing but judicial blindness on the part of Christians, sincerely so, who consent weakly to the withdrawal of barrier after barrier which the wisdom of the past has set up to keep out the deluge of infidelity, which has been fostered and produced by the agency chiefly of the cheap printing press. What kind of an outcome we may look for from a perfectly Godless democracy may be inferred from the following, which appeared in the *Daily Telegraph* of December 10, 1888 :—

" The Anarchists' *vade-mecum*, or ' Dynamite Guide,' is the dangerously fascinating title of a volume which has been printed somewhere in the neighbourhood of Leicester Square, London, and is at present circulating among the discontented *compagnons* of Paris. The book is written in the simplest style, so that it may be thoroughly 'understanded of the people,' and may enable them to profit by its instructions in the hour of 'the approaching conflict with sweaters and oppressors.' The compiler of the *Indicateur* in his introduction, makes a strong appeal to all *compagnons* who are without weapons, and then launches into a long detail of the various explosives which may be used in the time of action. Among these are 'Fenian fire,' which is reputed excellent for throwing among policemen or cavalry; 'Lorraine fire,' 'suffocating bombshells,' 'explosive cigarettes,' 'sudden-death grenades,' and various other combustibles, the preparation of which with dynamite, nitro-benzine, and similar combustible materials, is lucidly described. With this terrible information are intermingled instructions in street-fighting and general revolutionary tactics. 'Gas' is to be used as an agent of destruction whenever dynamite is not procurable. All government buildings and public institutions which stand as symbols of oppression from the past are to be blown up, and thoroughly destroyed, and the people are told they should not listen to Parliamentary Socialists, who counsel calmness and moderation, but should act on their own initiative and with determination. The book bears the imprint of the 'Imprimerie Internationale Anarchiste de Londres,' and some of its contents are manifestly taken from the works of Herr Most."

But turning away from these revolting details, let us glance for a moment at some of the results that would spring from the substitution of a religious for a secular basis in State Education in Australasia. Clearly the net outcome would be an enormous increase in the virtue and practical sterling worth of the whole of the coming generation. The overwhelming majority of the new generation would be composed of persons who would be a law to themselves, and it would be shown triumphantly that if aught can regenerate and perfect man in this life it is Christianity, and that alone. Indissolubly united by the solidarity of religion, the great Anglo-Saxon communities of the Southern Cross would stretch across the world, resting on the United Kingdom; and the whole British Dominion, which might by well concerted action secure all the sea-borne trade of the nations, would then hold the whole ocean and keep it inviolate against the rest of the world. The flag of this great dominion would be that of peaceful industry and commerce—of a Christendom whose mission was to Christianise the rest of the world, and thus united in itself, its power to repel any attack would be absolutely unlimited. One hundred millions of Anglo-Saxons banded together under the ensign of a pure Theocratic Democracy would first control and afterwards dominate the world itself, and war, like other plagues of scientific infidelity and satanic free-thought, would disappear from the face of the globe, where virtually we should have in place of the existing political chaos of hate and jealousy and endless strife, a Paradise Regained of Christian brotherhood and love.

In one word it is indeed true that the service of God alone is perfect freedom, and not the service of man, as some vainly suppose. The following lines seem to me to express the whole Christian scheme very completely—

>Thy Kingdom come. Three words embody here
>The sum and substance of the Christian creed,

> All knowledge and all wisdom man can need—
> The Adam fallen from his sinless sphere,
> The Victor Adam on the Cross to bleed!
> Eternal King of David's chosen seed,
> Gethsemane restoring Paradise,
> And earth preparing for the beautiful,
> The pure, the holy theocratic rule
> That blessed in dreams the royal minstrel's eyes.
> For 'tis this earth, and not a sphere unknown,
> That purged by judgment, shall that Kingdom be,
> Where Christ shall build His everlasting Throne,
> And man be good, because completely free.

There can be no fruit without a flower and no flower without a seed, and without the sower, be it bird, wind or man, no initial to the final fruition. Without a deliberate and well-organised propaganda how can there be an all-prevailing Christianity; and without Christians how can there be a Christendom? If those who *have* religious convictions and who desire to see the Church of Christ triumphant, choose to give up all the great agencies and opportunities now before them to the eager Secularist, the Agnostic, the Scientist, and the professed Infidel, what can—what must they expect? Why, nothing short of complete and overwhelming defeat. Yes, say objectors who dread to be thought intolerant, but we have our churches and our Sunday schools and a great mass of missionary and evangelical machinery, and with this we must counteract the unbelieving tendencies of the day. Indeed, as well might a regiment surrounded by an enemy throw down its arms and then cry, *now* we can charge and break our way through! If the Secularist will not tolerate the Bible and the formula of prayer in the weekday schools of the State, do you suppose that in times to come he will tolerate it in any public form? If the Christian elects to take the back seat in the House where the government of peoples is carried on, depend on it that by and by he is sure to be deprived even of that, and will find himself turned out altogether by the future Cromwells of the great Freethought camp. Surely *if* Christianity *is* to be propagated—surely if there are still men and women sincerely anxious that the visible Kingdom of Christ should be established on this earth they must indeed be judicially mad and judicially blind to voluntarily yield every point of vantage and place an implacable enemy in full possession of school, parliament and university. To me it has always seemed amazing. If the Christian really believes what he professes, it is his obvious duty, and nothing less, to avail himself of *every advantage* that he can obtain to strive against the increasing torrent of infidelity which is loose among us. Take possession of the schools of the State, inculcate Christianity on the minds of all the future generation, leaven the coming Democracy with the sympathies, the charities and the enthusiasm of a militant Christianity, fence the Parliament absolutely against the entrance of any infidel *as* an infidel (if he comes in as a wolf in sheep's clothing the sin and the hypocrisy rest on him—not on you); insist that all public acts be publicly placed under the sanction of a theocratic State, and then, and only then, can you expect to create and to preserve a true Christendom.

If, on the other hand, believers aid the adversary, as they now do, by weakly retiring all along the fighting line, they will certainly see militant science finally enthroned with its intellectual despotism, which dares to appraise human life at relative values, and would, and will perhaps some day, condemn the pauper to vivisection to preserve a president of a British Association for the Promotion of Knowledge, to propagate a little longer practical Atheism under the specious cloak of a cultured and refined Freethought.

THE TREASURE TREE:

A ROMANCE OF NEW GUINEA.

I.—Seeking the Gold for a Wedding Ring.

"Sugar and gold, sweetness and wealth!" some new arrival exclaimed on the first sight of Maryborough, which lies northward 180 miles from Brisbane, the capital of Queensland, and is specially the outport of the famous Gympie goldfields. All around are the sugar plantations—a rolling prairie flashing up in emerald and gold, and cut off from the horizon by the dense bush. The whole scene is tropical.

As to the town, with its picturesque wooden bridge over the river, the longest bridge in the whole colony, its iron foundries, shipyard, and—significant industries—two distilleries and at least as many breweries, it was, at the time of which I am writing, a medley of mean houses, pretentious "stores" tricked out with attractive advertisement signboards, and here and there buildings presenting real architectural "elevations," while the Court House, one or two churches, sundry insurance offices, and the Post Office were, and still are, quite on a level with most metropolitan edifices of the kind.

A pale slender young man, in whom every townsman could recognise a "new arrival," and who was evidently conscious of being thus conspicuous, was proceeding to the Post Office, balancing a letter in his white, thin, artist-like hand, with the air of one uncertain whether he should post it or not.

Harold Medlicott, although a mere youth, had already inherited from fortune the legacy of a sad romance. He was an only son, carefully brought up by an eccentric but apparently fond mother, who was "nursing" a fortune for him which had been left under her control, together with an old-fashioned house in Kensington. Harold, having been trained only as a "gentleman," and kept as much under his mother's eye as possible, had formed an attachment for the daughter of a half-pay captain of Engineers, a man of good birth, who was resolved to see that his "motherless girl" married well, and particularly to a man of means. This attachment came to Mrs. Medlicott's knowledge in due course, and a series of "terrible scenes" ensued, ending in a complete rupture between mother and son, the former declaring that her money should go to hospitals before her boy should become, as she expressed it, the "prey of that bad, bold girl, whose father was quite as designing as herself."

Harold left his home during one of these tempests of maternal invective, and confided his troubles to his one bosom friend, Dick Welford, a clerk in a bank, who was, as Harold truly said, one of the best natured fellows in the world. Dick soon found that his friend was commercially fit for nothing, and although he had some of the qualifications of the recognised professions he was not really suited for any one of them, as far as practical work went. It happened that a member of the banking firm where Dick was employed—a Mr. Walcott—was about going out to Queensland, on certain financial business, and required a secretary and general factotum to accompany him. Dick, who was as energetic as he was enthusiastic in his friendship, procured the appointment for his friend, and even found the ways and means to start him on his way. We do meet, now and then, with real, disinterested friendship, and it deserves honourable record.

"I told them," observed Dick, "that you were like the late Lord Clyde, ready to start anywhere—not to-morrow, but *now*—and I made bold to get your portmanteau, and a few little things suitable to the tropics, and there they are"—pointing to a corner of his "den."

"Dear old Dick!" And although these were two contemporary young Englishmen, and not impulsive French students, they embraced and positively hugged each other. It is true, however, that they knew there was no one to see them!

As Harold now walked slowly to the Maryborough Post Office, he was going over mentally the last letter that Miss Hardynge had written to him, in which she said that their engagement, begun through impulse, was a mistake. For herself she should never marry, but she would not bind Harold to his promises, and she was sure that her father would never consent unless, indeed, Mrs.

Medlicott, Harold's mother, altered entirely in her demeanour towards both Harold and herself, that she would not estrange mother and son, and more to the same purpose.

Harold was too unversed in the ways of woman to interpret the one luminous sentence in which the writer of this melancholy letter declared she should never marry, and he had penned in response the following, which sufficiently explains the nature of the plight whereto, like many a " new chum," he now found himself reduced:—

"Maryborough.—Dearest Norma,—I have come thus far in search of the gold for the wedding ring I mean to bring you, but as yet not a grain have I found. The voyage was monotonous, an affair of eating and drinking it seemed to me principally, and Mr. Walcott was and is good at both! We had many emigrants, a picked class they told me, but to my mind a wretched lot estimated by what I had read about the early days of our Colonies —pretty pioneers of Empire, truly. Most were speculating as to what lodgings they would find on arrival, and what situations would be open to them. Such slavish dependence on others! I never hinted as much to dear Dick, but you know my intense passion for liberty. The first chance I mean to start off and pick up my fortune, if it is lying about in this continent, or perish, and so trouble no one, not even you, dear, for I know you are at bottom as practical and sensible as I am poetic and sanguine. No man should drag down the girl he loves to a lower social scale, under the delusion of love in a cottage. What is this country like, you ask, to change a painful subject? This is a veritable land of rivers. The whole coast is cut up by them, coming down from the great mountains parallel to the shore. The scenery resembles somewhat Richmond Park indefinitely extended and a hundred times more beautiful. The trees, veritable towers of timber, stand well apart, and the herbage is the most luxuriant imaginable. To me it is like the 'setting' of some of the Arcadian scenes in the 'Faerie Queen,' while along the banks of the innumerable streams are thousands of flowering lilies.

"The purity of the air astonishes me. Nothing seemed stained or soiled. You may spend days out in the open air with clean face and hands, and as to the light it would bring joy to a photographer. As to the natives— I mean the settlers—they are, some of them, rough enough, and the new arrivals are to be pitied.

"'Where,' one of them grumbled, 'is the restaurant or even the coffee-house?' and so on. Truly Mr. Walcott said Queensland is not quite a country of hotels.

"Resuming this diary-like letter later, I find my fears confirmed as to Mr. Walcott's not being quite so amiable as dear Dick represented. The other day he remarked, 'Well, young man, it seems to me you are having a nice time. If you see any opening do not study me, but fill it. This is not a country where people can live on nothing a year!' What can have offended him? Although I thought of breaking away, this suddenness was not pleasant. I said I hoped I had not been remiss in my duties? 'Oh, no! your duties are well enough performed, seeing how confounded little they are! You ought never to have come out here. You are not the kind of man we want. By George, didn't I see you the other day attitudinising before an old gum tree and spouting like a London Cheap Jack, only not to such good purpose. Can you shear a sheep, whip up a mob of cattle, or put up a fence?'"

*   *   *   *   *

"Mackay.—This, dear Norma, is the very last of my letters, unless I can ever write to say 'I *have* found the gold for a wedding ring.' The crisis has come, and, as usual, the unforeseen has happened. My patron wears a loose coat like mine, and it chanced that, going out one blazing afternoon, I put on his by mistake. Before going far I discovered the error, and, further, that in one pocket was a bag heavy with gold. I was hastening back when some tremendous shouting and an evident disturbance attracted me onward, and made me oblivious of Mr. Walcott's gold. Outside a rough shedlike 'inn,' with the sign of 'The Gold Diggers' Arms,' was an uproarious group, the landlord in the midst, and by him a Hercules of a fellow with a great, laughing, red face, set off in a black frame of coarse hair, flourishing a slip of paper, and shouting, 'Come and drink, you devils!'

"I knew at once, from what had been told me before, that this was a miner who, paid for a spell of work with a cheque, had come to the inn deliberately to 'drink it out' by the ready aid of all the idle ruffians in the way. A common tub was brought out, a tin bowl placed at the side, and the landlord proceeded to empty a case of champagne into the tub. Unfortunately, I somehow attracted the notice of the man at whose expense this orgie was being given, and being in the benevolent stage of drunkenness, he yelled out, 'You, sir, Mr. Thirsty Face, come here and drink my health, and all the gentlemen's here!" And in a moment some of the ruffians clustering round had seized and were dragging me to the foaming tub. I turned, however, on my assailants with such an unexpected fury that I broke away, and, remembering at a flash the gold in my pocket, took to my heels, followed by the derisive jeers of the disreputable crew. Recovering breath, I felt for Mr. Walcott's bag of sovereigns. It had disappeared! Evidently some of the ruffians who had been foremost in this 'shouting' for drinks had robbed me. I felt I could never face Mr. Walcott, for an instinct told me he would never credit my story. My mind was made up. Mr. Walcott had gone that day to Amherst, north of the Pioneer River, on which Mackay stands, and would not return for some day or two. I have written a note explaining my misfortune and stating that I will relieve him of the burden of my maintenance, and that if I survive I will repay him the amount stolen. I then obtained a few rough necessaries, and am now about posting this the last of my letters proclaiming failure. Far away west lies the great dividing range, beyond which are well-watered plains with supposed auriferous plateau, all up to the Gulf of Carpentaria. I mean simply to tramp out northwards and accept my fate. It is, seriously speaking, better than suicide, my only other resource—a vulgar refuge—and your feelings will not be harrowed. And mark this, my dear, I love you none the less because you are practical and prudent, and a pattern daughter in love and filial obedience. I shall tramp on, I say. Providence will resolve whether I meet death or life in this march of mine. I go in search of gold. Others have found it, why not I? This is better, is it not, than dependence on others? My hope is in the chapter of accidents. I go, Norma. Farewell! If I write again you will know that the gold for your wedding-ring has been found in Australia. If I remain silent long you will know I am dead. Do not mourn. Forget. It is best."

II.—The Coral Sea.

One of the many physical marvels of the Austral ocean is undoubtedly the great Coral Sea, thus called from the substance of its innumerable reefs, extending, more or less, from the New Hebrides to the Queensland coast of Australia. Here and there are enormous stretches of banks lying at no great depth under the surface, and presenting, thanks to their vivid and varied colours, the beautiful similitude of natural submarine flower gardens. The Coral Sea is a region of natural wonders; one of its main features is the Great Barrier Reef, extending off the Queensland shores all the way up to Torres Straits, and including one reef which stretches for full 350 miles without the cleavage of a single channel.

It was early morning. Far up on the shores of the Coral Sea, beyond Cooktown, the growing glow of the rapidly advancing tropical sunshine revealed a scene of surpassing loveliness and appalling solitude. The air was still, except where it already began to quiver in a gathering haze of heat. Just here the shore was covered with luxuriant vegetation. The wild nutmeg hung out its pear-like golden fruit, while cedars and palms gave dignity and grace to the undulating lowlands that dipped their emerald edges, as it seemed, into an almost unrippled sea, stretching out into blue distances.

Suddenly the still life of the mingled landscape and seascape was illustrated in a double and very startling manner. From the south a boat abruptly shot into view, with only one man on board, who, after giving ever and anon a vigorous pull at his oars, rested back on his seat, and let his vessel glide on with its own impetus through the smooth and transparent waters that scarcely made an audible plash on the pebbly beach which occasionally broke the outline of the richly-wooded coast. Almost at the moment that the boat came thus into view at this particular part of an uninhabited shore, there was a crashing among the brushwood, and another man burst blindly out, amid a shower of leaves and torn branches, and rushed straight into the sea. It was here very shallow, and he struggled on a considerable distance before the lazy lap of the waves was above his waist. As though to complete the dramatic character of the double coincidence, a horrible, inarticulate, but human-like clamour broke from the dense foliage, and then a number of creatures, looking very like pantomimic sprites without the tinsel, came into full view, brandishing and darting their spears after the fugitive, who, dazed and breathless, yet saw the boat and its solitary occupant, and as the water deepened suddenly, struck out with frantic haste. Just as he sprawled on the waters, however, he was struck by a spear better aimed than half-a-dozen others that fell about and even beyond him.

The episode passed in a flash, but the solitary voyager took it all in at a glance. With a powerful turn of the wrist, he shot his boat towards the swimmer, and then, as two or three of the blacks dived in to pursue the escaping man and rose to the surface, a pistol went crack! 'crack! and the foremost tossed up his arms, yelled, and sank. The others hesitated, and the stranger, with a really marvellous vigour, rowed to the swimmer, seized him, and with one quick, powerful arm lifted him over the stern into the boat. Then, without a word, he bent to the oars and rowed off the shore with a speed that was as amazing as his own mixture of the imperturbable with the energetic and impulsive.

The two or three blacks who had taken to the water lost heart, and contented themselves with fishing up their comrade and dragging him back to the shore a limp, helpless mass, and in a few moments more the boat with its two occupants was out a considerable distance, and then, and not until then, the rescuer shipped his oars, and turning to the wounded man, who lay for the moment panting and helpless at the bottom of the boat, remarked, with a slight foreign accent:

"An introduction nearly as abrupt as your English manners. Eh, my friend?"

Harold, for it was he, looked up, and extending his hand, said: "You have saved my life. I thought it was gone this time, and, and ——," but the pain and loss of blood from his wound overcame him, and he swooned away.

"That is well," grunted the benevolent stranger; "the

bleeding will stop, and I can see what is the matter, eh?"

It appeared that Harold had received a severe flesh wound in the thigh, but the artery had fortunately escaped, and, having dressed the gash in a rough but skilful manner, the stranger produced a small flask and poured some of its contents, a particularly powerful cognac, down Harold's throat. He revived immediately, and the two now regarded each other attentively.

They were in all ways remarkable contrasts. Harold was, it must be admitted, a most deplorable object. He was reduced to almost the condition of a skeleton, and the few rags of his clothing that still remained hung upon him as on a scarecrow. His cheeks were mere skin, and his temples exhibited terrible hollows, like those of an old man. He was excoriated almost all over by constant struggles through dense thickets, and he seemed in the last stage of exhaustion, as well he might, seeing that for some time past he had chiefly subsisted on the fruits indigenous to Queensland, known as the Herbert River cherry, and occasionally the native kamquat.

As to his rescuer, he too was a study, although in a very different way. He was a man apparently of 60, but probably older, vigorous, hard, and sinewy, rather under the middle size, but most strongly built, and having the limbs of an athlete on a reduced scale. His face was tawny, and his black, thick eyebrows contrasted strangely with the short, strong, white beard that had begun to grow upon the chin, which was evidently habitually shaved. His dress was a strange medley of the garb of a Roman Catholic priest and a common sailor, and about the whole man there was something at once inviting and yet repelling, something at once benevolent and yet sinister, while his eyes were piercing and small, set wide apart and shadowed by a corrugated brow; had his tarpaulin hat been off, the tonsure of the priest could have been seen. The boat was no less singular than its owner. The whole of the outside was covered with various small marine plants and animals, long tufts of seaweed trailed behind like pennons in the transparent sea, and the gunwale was worn by the action of the waves into ribs, such as you see in the sand just after the tide has gone out. There was but little on board beyond two small water casks and a bag which contained some remains of biscuit, while in the bottom lay a crowbar, an axe, and sundry tools, together with a small box. A mast, designed to carry a small sail, now furled around it, also occupied the bottom of this mysterious boat, which, to Harold, had dropped, as it were, out of the sky.

The young man and the old man eyed each other for a full minute. Each look said plainly, "What do you do here?"

Presently the old man spoke.

"If I had not done with such things, I should certainly think that there was a Providence, after all. I have been wanting a companion for the last thousand miles or so, and lo! the land casts him forth into my very lap."

"And why," asked Harold, "should you doubt it now? I have been trying to kill myself these three months past, and have, as you see, miserably failed. Henceforth I believe in Providence."

III.—The First Hint of the Treasure.

Both these men were fugitives, although in widely different ways. For some days Harold's wound kept him prostrate, and he passed most of the weary time in the bottom of the boat. His strange companion nursed him with a singular care, and, after a few hours, these two beings—fated to meet in such a strange way, amid the solitude of the Coral Sea—had become, conversationally at least, familiar friends. Out in the primitive world of Nature there are no conventionalities, although there may be, all the same, secrets; and it was not long before Harold knew all about his companion that the latter chose to communicate to him; while, as to Harold, he had told his story in a very direct and simple way.

Succinctly put, what Harold learned amounted to this. His rescuer called himself Claud Dubec, and, by his own showing, he was a recidivist from New Caledonia, only, he explained, that all the "crimes" of which he had been accused were merely political. In New Caledonia he had enjoyed, in common with most of his companions in misfortune, much local freedom. It happened that some considerable time before undertaking his perilous voyage in an open boat, a compatriot, who fell sick, had been nursed by Dubec, who possessed a practical knowledge of medicine and surgery, as well as sundry other useful accomplishments, and in due course, believing him to be a priest—which in reality Dubec was not, although for purposes of his own he had assumed that character—made a confession to him just before the disease proved mortal, which had, as Dubec admitted, been the cause of his extraordinary action in committing himself to an open boat and the ocean with all its many risks. "The fact is," Dubec explained to Harold, "I am in search of a certain treasure in New Guinea, and if I find it my fortune is made." He then went on to say that he could easily have found companions to escape with him, for the authorities took little heed of the ordinary recidivists, and rather encouraged than otherwise their endeavour to reach Australia, but the whole of those he knew were, he admitted, such scoundrels that he dared not trust one of them, and in escaping, his principal anxiety was not so much to baffle the perfunctory search of the authorities as to evade his fellow convicts. For some days, however, he had been lamenting the want of a companion, for he had almost worn himself out by reason of reducing his sleep to short snatches, and, once in New Guinea, it was, he remarked, a serious thing to sleep without a look-out for the natives, and he sent rather a thrill through Harold by telling him of the mancatcher invented by the natives of Hood Bay, but now to be met with all over the vast expanses of New Guinea. This is simply a loop of rattan cane, the constant companion of the Head Hunters. A sharp spike is inserted in the handle, and the loop being once dexterously cast over the head of the victim a violent pull brings the spike into play, and usually drives it into the base of the skull or into the spine, with fatal effect.

At the first moment he recognised Harold as an Englishman, and he had speedily made up his mind to propose giving him a share of the treasure, if they found it, as a recompense for such service as Harold could render him in the work of its recovery.

Things had reached this point when Dubec, who had nearly cured the wound that Harold had received while escaping from the blacks, asked him plainly what his views were as to a division.

The colloquy that ensued was somewhat remarkable, illustrating as it did the character of this singular exile.

Harold was now feeling comparatively strong. Lately they had feasted on fish and on some parrots, while only the day before a young dugong, whose flesh is, when properly prepared, quite as good as bacon, had fallen to their lot.

"What do you want for your share if you help me to find and carry off this treasure?" Dubec asked.

"That depends on the amount of treasure and the work involved in getting it," Harold answered, with a smile.

"English all over, and thoroughly shopkeeper-like," replied Dubec, who spoke English with little perceptible accent, and with wonderful accuracy. "But you know that, but for me, you could find nothing, and, so far, it appears from your own showing, that you have been unfortunate in everything you have undertaken. I tell you there is a treasure somewhere in New Guinea. Well, what then? Can you find it? Go and try. I will land you there and leave you, if you like."

"I think you mean to take me with you all the same," said Harold, with a confident smile.

"Perhaps I do, but I want to have a proper understanding. Say, will you be content with value to the amount of five thousand?"

Harold opened his eyes. "It is a large treasure," he thought, and he felt that Norma was imperceptibly but surely coming at last within his reach. Dubec watched him intently, a scarcely noticeable sneer curling his lip as he went on—"Well, I see you think that amount too little. Will you be really content with ten thousand pounds?"

Harold started. His colour went and came, and his "Oh, yes!" was rather gasped than articulated. "Very well," remarked Dubec; "my friend, shake hands on that, and pledge me your word that whatever you see you will be content with that amount. Is it so?"

"It is;" and, added Harold, with simple earnestness, "I promise."

"I take your word, my friend; and do you know why?"

"No; how should I?"

"Because I have noticed that you pray morning and night when you fancy I am not looking at you. I frankly wish I could; but it is useless. I tell you so much that you may know what kind of man I am. I know, too, that my saying so much will not make any difference to you, except to cause your English conscience to cry out 'How shocking!' You will keep your belief, and I my unbelief. That is all. I trust you, my friend. Shake hands again. You will go back to your English miss with a small fortune, and I shall have the treasure. If I had brought any of my rascal compatriots with me they would have wanted the whole, and we should have had Murder before Discovery."

All this time the boat was making way, often aided by the sail when it seemed safe to set it, towards Torres Straits. Whenever there was the least sign of a vessel in the horizon, Dubec altered his course, and probably escaped all notice, as it is difficult to discern a small boat at sea at any considerable distance.

Their course was made for the north coast of New Guinea, which is remarkably rocky, and, even now, for the most part entirely unexplored. But when first the mountain tops of the great island came into view, Dubec decided to touch the shore as soon as possible, as he wanted a supply of fresh water, and hoped to procure some vegetables and fruit, the former being, as he explained to Harold, the taro. This is the name given in Polynesia to an edible root, quite a foot long, and capable of furnishing an agreeable food, while the leaves are accounted, when boiled, as equal to spinach.

All this while Dubec had merely generalised in regard to the "Treasure," and as at times he spoke very strangely and in a singular, abrupt way, Harold had some secret misgivings as to whether his companion was really quite right in his intellect. Not unfrequently, when he supposed Harold was sleeping, he would break forth into snatches of verse, always in French, and although Harold's acquaintance with that language was very imperfect, he gathered enough from his companion's utterances to ascertain that these effusions were addressed to the Genius of Political Liberty, and related generally to what Dubec called the coming Emancipation of Man from all forms of Law, Divine and Human.

IV.—The Legend of the Treasure Tree.

Like the eastern shores of North Australia, New Guinea is a land of numerous rivers, streams and brooklets; and some of these, issuing from natural groves of mango trees, are most picturesque interruptions to the beach and cliff, which latter is frequently very precipitous. The mango is a fine spreading tree, dividing a little over the height of a man into branches with foliage so dense that even the piercing rays of the tropical sun are shut out, and, hung all over with its sweet, luscious fruit, is at once a banquet and a sylvan hall to the wanderer in these regions.

Dubec and Harold had safely stretched across Torres Straits, and were now coasting cautiously in a westerly direction, with a view to gaining the unexplored regions of the north of the island. Up to the present only a very few natives had been sighted, and these at a great distance. On this day Dubec had been hardy enough to run the boat up a lonely creek, arched over with dense foliage, while the banks were thickly grown with mango trees. Here, in the heat of the mid-day, they were now resting. Harold sat in the stern, watching the banks of the clear stream, on which the boat was pleasantly rocking, while Dubec lay at his ease in the bottom. Harold was evidently not at his ease. For one thing, he could not keep his mind from dwelling on a memory-picture of a certain day in far-off England, when he and Dick had discussed their joint prospects in life. What an appalling change, he thought, between now and then!

"Melancholy, as usual," observed the Frenchman. "Evidently thinking of the English miss!" Then, as Harold did not reply, he went on, "Possibly you doubt the Treasure. Possibly you think me a madman. Well, you shall see. Meanwhile, my friend, let me tell you the way to be happy is this—care for no one but yourself; avoid all attachments; be tranquil. Look at me;" and he paused with an evident sense of inward exultation, continuing, "See how I have come up after every fight with Fortune. I am three times your age and more, and have all my teeth, and such a digestion. Even these pigeons and old parrots cannot try it."

Harold made some commonplace rejoinder, but he could not help thinking that M. Dubec had not much to boast of in finding himself a recidivist in his old age. It is probable that this reflection was pretty legibly written on the lad's ingenuous countenance, for his companion went on, in a moralising tone—

"Ah! you say—but how comes it you go into exile? I answer, Destiny. It is magnificent, for it leads me to the treasure which will buy me pleasure, youth, long days, flattery, power, and—Revenge." The old convict twisted his mouth into an ominous grimace, and added— "But you are asking what of this treasure—where is it? Now I tell you. Listen. You know, my friend, that there is near Bombay a city called Goa; it is Portuguese. It is a city of the Pope, of monks, and nuns. Well, more than fifty years ago, you—I mean your countrymen— were at war, and you boast of your Wellington, your Nelson. Good; but there was another side to that, and in the Indian Ocean we take your ships, your merchandise, and get glory and gain—much gain. One of our smallest ships was commanded by a very young man —a child like you; he had been of the old *noblesse*, and he was devout, brave, great. I take off my hat to him, I admire him, and I see him now. All went well with him until he had the misfortune to conceive a grand passion for—ah! what do you think? Why, a nun in a convent at Goa. She was not a common nun, either; her family had power and wealth, and the pride of the Pope. My friend carried this nun off by force and strategy, and then he found himself in great peril. He was pursued, and he fled into more eastern seas, and, before long, in his wrath, turned a veritable pirate. He had two lives henceforth, my friend—one all ferocity and greed, the other all gentleness and devotion. His great aim was to hide his mistress away where no one could find her, and he discovered a place on the north side of Papua where the navigation is most dangerous.

" He formed a retreat near the coast, and only four of his crew knew where it was. After the work was done, he used to lie off with his vessel and row himself alone through the channel he had found, and return in a given time the same way. It is curious that the four men who helped him to form the retreat I have told you of were all killed soon after in a variety of ways. I don't know the precise particulars, but I believe two of them at least were shot in the back during some of the many engagements he fought in the China seas.

" It was known that he had hidden the nun away somewhere in Papua, and that he periodically visited her there. That was all. Meanwhile, he was more daring and yet more cautious than ever in his piracies, and he began to accumulate treasure. Do you understand, my friend? What was his object? I will tell you. He resolved to amass a fortune in a portable form, and he quietly exchanged away his share of the plunder he obtained—much of it silver dollars—for gold and diamonds, sapphires, and other gems. There he was right enough. It is no bad thing to invest in precious stones—a fortune takes up such a small amount of room! The diamond at least is not fickle, and it never deceives! It is hard and cold, but it is true to its owner. Meanwhile, however, as you may imagine, matters in this Papuan retreat were not exactly satisfactory to this very adventurous and unfaithful nun. Philippe—that is the name of this convent spoiler—provided, I believe, a Papuan damsel as an attendant on his lady love. Well, to shorten a long story, things seem to have gone badly in this romantic sylvan retreat. My friend Philippe prospered exceedingly as a gentleman pirate, and was the idol of his crew—a very small one, by the way, but as fine a set of Bretons as ever sailed. Had he had the sense to stick to his conversion of silver dollars into diamonds, rubies and sapphires, and merely found a sylvan asylum for them, all would have gone well with him; but he had bound himself to a woman who, wretched as a nun, seems to have mourned over her convent as soon as she left it, and to have been seized with what are called, I believe, qualms of conscience—some derangement, depend on it, my friend, in the digestion. What was the result? First of all Philippe had qualms in *his* conscience, and he began to be haunted by nightmares of an angry and, indeed, infuriated Mother Church, and he resolved to amass just a little, only a little more, and then abandon the trade and carry off his repentant nun to America, and go virtuously into broadcloth and silk, tall hats and Paris bonnets, and live respectably and 'cleanly,' as, I think, your divine 'Williams' has it, ever after. Such was Philippe's idea, but any man who devotes himself to a woman gives all the odds to fortune, and the nun who had wrought all this mischief—diverting a French gentleman and a hero from a patriot to a pirate—took such a fit of melancholy that she died, and on visiting his sylvan asylum, after a very profitable cruise, Philippe found the mistress dead and the maid flown into the bush. What did he do? Did he, like a wise man, bow to the inevitable course of human vicissitudes? Did he recover his treasure and steal away alone to civilisation and enjoyment—to safety and reputation? Oh no! He went mad for a time, and, having shut up his sylvan home, where he could never, to my thinking, have enjoyed himself very much, he fled away without a single gem, and did not even return to his brave compatriots. He sank into poverty, and eventually worked his way back to France as a common sailor, and sought out his Breton home. That home had disappeared, like so many more indeed, before the flood of war, and Philippe dragged on a wretched existence for years, eaten up with remorse for his piracies, and especially for his horrible sacrilege. Well, you are beginning to guess the sequel. He fell across my path, and we had a mutual liking—and, indeed, I liked Philippe very much. He confessed all to me, and expressed his fear as to whether he ought not to have recovered the treasure and given it to the Goa convent whence he ravished the nun who had been his ruin! I do not know whether he might not have eventually carried out this altogether insane idea, but he died suddenly, leaving me the legacy of his remorse and his secret. I need not say more. I kept my knowledge of the Treasure Tree to myself, and waited until an opportunity offered for escaping alone. Long before I had reached the Coral Sea, I began to regret that I had come alone, although I honestly confess that I do not know one of my late companions in exile whom I could have trusted while I slept, as I am going to now, my friend." And so saying, the speaker folded his arms across his chest, turned over on his side, and in a few moments very audibly slept, while Harold remained motionless and lost in thought at his end of the boat, which, still gently rocking up and down, seemed to be in rhythmical accordance with a vision that had sprung up before his half-shut, dreaming eyes, of Norma as he had last seen her in that far-off typical English home.

V.—A Papuan Forest.

Land mist and sea foam. All along the shore luxuriant vegetation, half hidden in a quivering haze of moist heat, and strangely illuminated here and there by the vivid hues of tree-borne flowers. Up and up, mountain and vegetation soar together, a wondrous irregular slope of all shades of green, variegated with all the hues of the rainbow, and blending a tlast with the blazing sky of a tropical day. All below, at the foot of this fruitful shore, boomed and beat an almost tempestuous sea, churned into vast fountains of irridescent spray, occasioned by the dashing of the heavy seas amid the tortuous passages of innumerable rocks and reefs which every moment threatened the boat of our two adventurers with immediate destruction. The earth, air, sea and sky were all blended together in a blinding, overpowering beauty. In some places along the shore, where the low-lying reefs threw up the greatest abundance of spray and the haze of the land heat was thickest, in a sort of half-luminous steam, the projection on high of what appeared an air-born Eden of surpassing loveliness had a startling effect, while everywhere there were innumerable flights of birds, and, as the boat slowly drew near the shore, Dubec and Harold were stirred into a burst of involuntary admiration and wonder as a cloud of birds of paradise floated by, far up in the glowing sky, the indescribably beautiful play of colours in their lovely plumage giving them all the appearance of air-born creatures arrayed in living sunbeams, and expressing with each movement the very essence of physical joy and brightness.

Never had Harold imagined, although he had read as much about the tropics as most young men of his age and station, that there could be concentrated within one sweep of the human vision such a wealth of colour—such a splendour of pure light, and such an intense profusion of life, in what seemed to him a Paradisiacal region. The palms, in particular, as they drew nearer still, were amazing for their magnitude, some of the leaves being indeed full fifty feet long, while the powerful odour of some of the flowers attracted dense clouds of insects. Oranges and lemons, loaded with fruit, could also be distinguished, together with the cocoanut and the masooi, whose fragrant bark exhales a delightful and powerful scent.

Several times Harold lost himself so far in his spontaneous admiration of the gorgeous scene that Dubec called him sharply to his senses, as once or twice the boat was well nigh swamped with the breakers, and at other times bumped and grated on the rocks, as they came on with the powerful inrolling tide to a kind of crescent bay, surrounded and guarded by tremendous cliffs, over which in several places there dashed down, in mighty cascades, the mountain streams that found here an outlet for their waters.

Dubec seemed puzzled; and he grew at once excited and angry, speaking rapidly in French to himself, and in a manner quite unintelligible to his companion. Suddenly he gave vent to a jubilant ejaculation, and, throwing himself into the stern of the boat, burst into a fit of laughter, which Harold plainly regarded as idiotic.

"Ah!" exclaimed Dubec, recovering his usual demeanour, "you cold, icy English, you have no sympathy —you have no *esprit*—you do not know what it is to imagine. I have seen my fortune at last—(sinking his voice to a low whisper)—I have seen the *place of the tree;* now we go on—we are in the right passage, and my friend Philippe, he tell the truth."

Harold, of course, saw nothing in the way of a landmark, and remarked, drily, that he should like to see the place too.

"All in good time," replied Dubec; "you would not know or understand if I showed you. We shall presently find ourselves in a creek, and then in a little river, and then—and then, my friend—we shall see, we shall see a sight—a magnificent sight!"

It certainly turned out so, for, in accordance with Dubec's prediction, in a short time they were borne by the strong current into a small creek, which looked very like a natural dock, the sides rising abruptly; and after pulling vigorously for a while, they entered first a deliciously green twilight, caused by the trees meeting overhead, shot here and there with sunshine; and as they proceeded further up a narrowing stream the gloom deepened, and in front, as overhead, for the most part there closed an extraordinary mass of the most luxuriant vegetation, so dense that it seemed impossible to land without cutting out standing room from among the inextricable tangle of grasses, reeds, plants and trees, all bound together with intricate masses of climbing vegetation. All was vigorous vitality—no dead thing could be seen. From the water's edge to the very crown of the beautiful green and blossom-and-fruit-variegated tunnel through which they forced the boat, everything was exuberant and fragrant, and, as Harold soon found, to his great disgust at first, the insect life was in proportion to the extraordinary wealth of vegetation, which here throve in an atmosphere of 80 or 90 degrees, although entirely shielded from the rays of the sun. After a while exertion became far too painful to be persisted in, and both rested on their oars and looked at each other exhausted.

"Ah! you see what a tropical forest is like now,"

remarked Dubec, who was evidently the less overcome by the effects of the vapour bath in which they floated. "Wait a while; we shall find that Master Philippe chose cooler quarters further up. I wonder, my friend, what your English miss would say to such a place as this? How would it do for what you call, I think, a picnic?"

"Not at all," gasped Harold; "I think I would rather the next time seek a treasure at the North Pole. Can't say I like adventures, now I am in for them at last. I can tell you, old man, if we do get out of this mess, as it seems to me, I shall have no more adventures, I can promise you."

"And yet," rejoined Dubec, in a musing tone, "the life has its good side, if we can only escape the head-hunters. There is nothing to do but to enjoy. All you really want is furnished ready. The sago tree, for example, is a regular natural flour mill, and when it has reared its pithy tower full of flour it is ready to build another for anyone who will kindly cut down its pillar of natural flour barrels, piled one on the other! I have had many adventures, and look for many more, but I suppose you will return to your domestic monotone—your getting up to breakfast, read the newspaper, talk, write, gossip, dine, smoke perhaps, and then the comfortable bed again, and the dull, correct, proper English wife. Bah! it is a very insipid business."

"Insipid or not, I should be very glad to be back again in London," Harold replied, emphatically; "and, what is more, I should never have come out if I had known what was before me."

"Not even for the fortune?"

"Well, we haven't got it yet."

"Ah, that is sure! But you astonish me. You are not the English youth I have heard and read of, but never seen. I wonder what you would do for me if we were to run into a nest of savages? They may be anywhere about us, and a flight of arrows would be very awkward here."

"Oh, you will find me quite ready to fight," rejoined Harold; "only I mean to say I have just had enough of this life, and I don't want any more of it. Give me England for ever, a steady business, and a good wife. I never knew till now all the blessings that such common things really meant."

Dubec regarded the young man attentively, and with an evident sneer that ended in a mocking smile, as he exclaimed, "One life—one love—how exceedingly ridiculous? Did you ever hear of Lope Felix de Vega-Carpio? Ah! what is your divine Williams to him? He began a soldier, then half turned priest—that was useful by way of experiences—figured at Madrid, went into court life, married a great lady, Isabella de Urbino, quarrelled with a courtier, satirised and then killed him in a duel. Lope next had a turn in prison—more useful experiences, my boy—and lost his wife, and, for a little while, had a new luxury, lucky fellow, that of grief. Next we find Lope serving in the Armada, which was beaten, my friend, by the storm and the sea—not by the English, mark you; and returned to Madrid. Lope there became secretary to some of the leading statesmen of the day—and what a day it was!— and again married. He lived happy, and had a son! Lo and behold! wife and son died; but he soon found consolation with Donna Maria de Luxan, and, when he was once more quite tired out with pleasure, he became a priest in earnest, and entered the Order of St. Francis in 1609, and such was his ardour that he burnt a heretic in 1623. I tell you Lope lived in splendour when he chose, and when he preferred to be the hermit he found the alternative good. Why, he grew so great that people used to talk of a Lope jewel or a Lope poem. He wrote nearly two thousand plays, and sometimes he composed a whole drama in one single day! No one was ever like him. Your Shakspeare—bah! he was nowhere. I say this was a man; but you, with your English notions—your one love, one wife, one home, one occupation—bah! again. You do not live, you do not see the world, and you do not understand men and women either—you are wretched—what you call it—nincompoop."

"I don't know anything about your hero, but if he had lived among us I fancy he would have been hanged," retorted Harold, who of late had—he hardly knew why—felt an increasing distrust of, and dislike to, his companion. He had, to tell the plain truth, been greatly exercised within himself to account for what he conceived to be Dubec's generosity in regard to the Treasure. It had dawned on him by a kind of intuition that Dubec was mocking him throughout—that circumstances having cast him in the way of the Frenchman, the latter was willing to make what use he could of his aid, and that if, when the Treasure (if it really existed, which he sometimes doubted) was found, Dubec could dispense with his services, Harold would find himself left in the lurch, if—

as a dreadful instinct warned him—the old recidivist did not imitate the action of his friend Philippe, who, he shrewdly suspected, like other pirates on like occasions, had already assassinated the men who knew of the locality of his treasure. Altogether Harold felt particularly uncomfortable, and the more so as he was practically unarmed, while Dubec carried—but where did not appear —a pistol which had already done execution on the Queensland blacks. In addition to this intense disquietude, Harold felt all the time that the old convict had undoubtedly saved his life, and in a strange, almost inexplicable, way there was mingled in his mind a profound sense of gratitude with an utter distrust.

As they floated further up the stream, which wound in and out amid what was in fact an impenetrable forest, the water began to fail them, and they were continually grounding. The only resource was to get out and push the boat off, and sometimes propel it for weary distances through a dreadful black ooze with but a few inches of clear water above, and, as Harold expressed it to himself, with a constant apprehension of treading on some venomous reptile finding its home in the rotting vegetation that seemed to form the bed of the rivulet.

Happily, Papua, unlike Borneo, has little in its forests of a noxious kind, and beyond bats and a few tree-climbing kangaroos, they encountered nothing living besides the innumerable birds and the complete plague of insects which sorely tried the temper of Harold. At length the rivulet began to run so dry that Dubec proposed to leave the boat, it being evidently useless toil to carry it further, and, moreover, as Dubec now condescended to inform his companion, they must be nearing the end of their toilsome journey, "unless," as he muttered to himself, "my friend Philippe was the victim of some opium dream."

As the stream narrowed and grew more and more indistinct, it being difficult to trace its bed at times, Dubec's spirits evidently rose. It was quite evident that he was all the while following a very complete clue, with the details of which he did not choose to trouble Harold; and, indeed, although ever and anon he broke forth into various gay *chansons* which he never quite finished, always starting a new one after a verse or two had rippled forth from a mouth that ill-suited such airy trifles, he hardly addressed a word to Harold, who trudged on by his side, wrapped in thought that seemed to grow more gloomy in proportion as Dubec became obviously more gay. At last, just as the bed of the stream seemed to disappear altogether, and a dense, impenetrable mass of verdure, solid as a wall, rose up before them, the old recidivist grasped his companion's arm with a hand which quivered with the strength of his emotion, and stopped abruptly, exclaiming in French, "It is here." The manner an the tone roused Harold from the lethargy which seemed to have crept over him, and pulling himself together with an effort, he rejoined, "Then it is about time, for it is my belief that I am going to be knocked over by some confounded fever or disease peculiar to this awful vapour bath."

"Nonsense!" cried Dubec. "We shall soon cure that; the treasure is in sight, almost; at all events, the Tree is." And taking a strong hold of Harold's arm, as though at this particular moment he feared desertion, he plunged with him into the thick undergrowth on the right, and presently, after battling with innumerable creepers, the two emerged on a small glade or opening, to which, in truth, a kind of avenue had been originally cut, but which was now nearly choked up by the rank vegetation that had sprung up to fill the place of a long line of felled trees, forming a kind of timber road, over which they stumbled with no little difficulty.

"There," said Dubec, pointing straight in front; "there is the Tree. Whether we shall find the treasure too, may be another thing."

But the sight that met their view—the day was now drawing to a close—must be reserved for another chapter.

VI.—Inside the Tree.

The sight that the two explorers beheld was, indeed, arrestive. They stood on the verge of a small glade, walled in by the loftiest and mightiest trees that had yet met their view—trees that soared up over a hundred feet at least, and from which depended fantastic curtains, as it were, of climbing plants, many having aërial roots, clinging to the topmost boughs of the trees, and some being gorgeous with flowers of gigantic size and of colours which were, even in the fast-failing light, singularly vivid. Harold was no botanist, and knew nothing of trees and plants beyond what he had picked up from his knowledge of English gardens and parks; but Dubec pointed out, as the cause of a peculiar odour which loaded the air, some camphor trees, massive in trunk and having small yellowish-white flowers. And there were, too, some splendid ironwood trees, which, with their enormous masses of flowers, very like small white roses, in striking contrast with the deep crimson buds and shoots of this remarkable tree, lighted up the glade in a manner at once beautiful and yet ghastly. Dubec informed his companion that this species of Myrtaceæ, which includes the clove and the eucalypti, is planted frequently near Buddhist temples, on account of their equable and enduring fragrance. All this, which takes many words to faintly depict, was seen at a glance; but the attention of both was fascinated by a single tree, which Harold, without a word more from his strange companion, felt instinctively must be the object of their long and painful search. It was of gigantic girth, and rose to a giddy height without throwing out a single branch; but, at an elevation at which everything was now dim and indistinct, there spread out an immense head of thick foliage, which loomed like a grotesque airborn structure—for it had a certain defined form—in the gathering obscurity.

The tree, which was altogether the vastest they had yet encountered, was very far from occupying the centre of the clearing, but its branches, which spread a considerable distance, and stretched out quite horizontally at one point, appeared in contact, and to be even intermingled, with the foliage of one or two of the trees on that side of the glade nearest to this veritable giant of the Papuan forest.

Neither of our adventurers at first approached within

several yards of the tree. Harold felt an inward awe that he could not explain, and Dubec, now that the goal was attained, had grown marvellously quiet and complacent. The fact was, now the tree stood before him exactly as it had been described in Philippe's confession, he hesitated on the eve of the final investigation, for the dreadful thought flashed through his mind—Suppose that after all the treasure is not there! But he preserved an outer calm, and even sought excuse, as it were, to postpone for a time the crucial investigation.

"Yes, my friend," he said, "that is the tree unquestionably, and up there, where that mass of branches and leaves look so solid, is the lofty sylvan mansion—the country seat, I think you English call it—of my foolish friend."

" It is a tree house then?" observed Harold, who had heard of the tree houses of New Guinea, although, owing to their remarkable success so far in keeping clear of the natives, they had not yet seen a specimen of this extraordinary form of human dwelling.

" Yes, my friend, it is a tree house, but one of a very peculiar kind, as you will soon see. These houses have usually ladders with long vines at each side, an abundance of natural cordage to get up by, and these black fellows manufacture first-rate ladders, broad as a staircase and nearly as easy to go up; here there is nothing of the kind, but the house is up there (pointing with his hand) all the same."

" I suppose," said Harold, in his matter-of-fact, commonplace manner, " that the ladder was there, but it has simply decayed and rotted away among this rank grass."

"No, my friend, you are wrong. These ladders require sentinels at the top to see who climbs up, but our friend Philippe had a better idea than that. Bah! He was clever—an original. I tell you he put his ladder inside the tree, and laughed at the savages, the head-hunters, and all the rest. Oh, he beat all—except destiny."

Some little time had elapsed since our two explorers had first penetrated into this strange glade, and it was now not only dark but beginning to be decidedly chilly, for even in New Guinea—island of an Orient sun as it is—the nights are cold, and many of the natives have the practice of keeping a fire going in their huts during the period of slumber—a thing that is at once a comfort and a precaution, for it operates as a good prophylactic against the noxious vapours that exhale from the enormous masses of undergrowth and rank weeds in a country where hardly a spot can be found clear of vegetation of the rankest sort.

"Come," continued Dubec, "let us have a fire and some supper and a light, and then we can see what is before us."

Both were, indeed, physically very tired with their long and laborious forced march up the difficult bed of the stream, which had, in reality, been the guide or clue to the mysterious tree, and the prospect of a fire, supper, and a little rest, was equally welcome to each. A quantity of dead wood was collected, and, a space being cleared near the tree by dragging up the grass, Dubec soon started a good fire with a pinch of gunpowder, and, having searched about a little, speedily brought a good supply of taro—a good esculent root, which when baked or roasted, forms a capital substitute for potatoes. A couple of parrots they had knocked over with sticks during their tramp up from the bay were roughly plucked, and in a surprisingly short time they had a fair meal ready. Presently Harold, having taken the edge off his appetite, observed:—" If anybody—you yourself—had told me that he could sit here quite quietly a few feet off a treasure tree, as you call it, and not go right mad with excitement, I should have declared it to be impossible."

"Ah!" replied Dubec drily, " I have seen men going to a new gold field act like lunatics until they arrived, and the sight of the expanse of common-looking land generally sobered them pretty much. There is no use for us to go into a fit because we are here. The tree is there, safe enough; the next thing is to get in it."

" Get in it?" inquired Harold, with genuine surprise. " I thought it had to be climbed."

"You wouldn't find that an easy job; and if the story is true we shall find that this tree is very like an old Breton tower that my old friend Philippe had in his mind when he chose this spot for his sylvan château. It has, or should have, a regular door and a zigzag sort of stair inside, going up to the dwelling part, which is built out on the branches, and which we cannot see now, on account of the darkness and the foliage."

Harold felt his heart begin to beat with a sinister agitation. The fever and fatigue of the toiling journey had deadened his finer perception, but now, as the legend narrated by Dubec recurred to his mind, in a somewhat confused shape, a strange, undefined fear possessed him, and he found his mistrust of his companion swallowed up in a growing horror of the tree itself, and of the dark and pent-up terrible secrets enclosed within it. A certain hesitation, too, seemed to have infected Dubec, who, after a rest by the fire, rose and walked about, approaching within a few feet of the tree, and then turning off abruptly. At last he ordered Harold to collect more fuel, and, aiding himself in this work, fed the fire and made it up somewhat nearer the tree, and so as to cast a powerful light on the whole of that side of the vast bole, which, thus illuminated, revealed, in the dry bark and gnarled appearance of the surface, signs of an antiquity that seemed quite in keeping with its enormous girth.

"We may be, after all, on the wrong side," remarked Dubec, "and if so must light up on the other, but there should be an opening here somewhere."

Then, to the intense wonderment of his companion, he began peering closely into the surface and feeling all over it with his hands, as though in search of some familiar object. At length he uttered an exclamation of delight, and, aided by Harold, one with a hatchet, the other with a knife, began scraping and laying bare the wood itself, and exposed to view a very palpable and perpendicular cut or cleft, that extended upwards about six feet, and after some further patient chopping, hacking, and scraping, a transverse cut was exposed to view also, and then a parallel perpendicular crack, thus revealing the parallelogram of a small door such as is sometimes found in the salient towers of mediæval castles. A careful examination and the use of a hatchet leverwise, which Dubec applied with all his strength, soon showed that the "door" consisted of a solid slice of the tree pivoted in very thick wooden pins at the top and bottom, and leaving, when this valve-like portal was fully opened, two rather slit-like entrances, which led to an interior of impenetrable darkness.

Dubec wiped the moisture from his face and forehead, for the exertion had been great, and he had refused, with an irritation not exhibited before, to accept Harold's aid. He was evidently growing dreadfully excited, though struggling to preserve a calm demeanour, while somehow Harold did not feel, as he had expected, at all elated now that the object of their search was before them.

"If that valve had jammed," remarked Dubec, "it would have been a big job; see, it is more than a foot thick at the least, and no doubt it was made in the thinnest part of the trunk. Now, before we go in, we must have lights, that is certain."

Harold suggested manufacturing some torches, or bringing the fire still nearer, so as to cast its radiance well into the opening. This last proposal Dubec rejected as fraught with peril, and he pointed out to Harold how old and dry the gigantic bole of this veteran of a tropical forest had become. "There is," he said, "if Philippe spoke truth, a hollow way right up to the house, and if we once had fire in such a shaft as that nothing could put it out. But we must have light to climb up, and, besides, there is no knowing what may be inside."

It struck Harold that, although the coveted treasure of glittering jewels had gleamed rainbow-like in the imagination of both while they were yet afar, it was a problem as to what would really be found, and he began to shudder within himself as he remembered that, whether a treasure-house or not, the tree was most certainly a tomb. So strong was this feeling that he could not forbear from saying to Dubec, "You seem to forget the dead."

"Oh! no, not at all, my young friend. But I do not fancy that will trouble us much. In a place like this the insects would soon leave nothing but bones. I only hope that nothing worse has happened. In these countries it is no uncommon thing to bury in trees, and the reptiles and the birds soon make everything fresh and sweet," and the old recidivist grinned a diabolical grin. Harold shrank back in undisguised disgust, and exclaimed that to his ears such words were profane and sacrilegious. "Oh!" said Dubec, with more sternness than sarcasm, for he was growing evidently more serious, and had lost his mocking manner, "I quite comprehend. You have scruples. You shall soon see, my brave, how many I have. Now come and help me to make some torches. It is no use torturing ourselves this way. Let us find the treasure, if it exists, and then we can argue as much as you please about sacrilege."

A terrible fit of gloom had seized on Harold. The whole scene—and the crisis had arrived—seemed to him a nightmare. Although Dubec had eaten freely of the rough food that the sea and the forest had yielded them, Harold had not even now become "seasoned" to such fare, and he was more debilitated than he himself knew, and the strain of helping to push the boat up the bed of the shallow stream had told severely on his nervous system; and just now, in the midst of the deep gloom of the mysterious glade and the fantastic shadows created by the flickering fire, he grew giddy, and it was only with a great effort that he succeeded in pulling himself together and assisting his companion in preparing some torches of twisted and resinous rattans which Dubec selected as likely to serve their purpose. When these were finished to his satisfaction he lighted one himself, and, bidding Harold light another and carry some spare bundles in case of need, our two adventurers stepped into the interior of the tree, and then, by common consent, paused at the strange sight that met their wondering eyes. The interior hollow was evidently in part the result of natural decay, and in part had been enlarged by the use of tools, and the orifice, which at the base might measure ten or twelve feet in diameter, seemed to contract overhead, but the feeble light of the rude torches, which emitted quite as much smoke as flame, entirely failed to light many feet upwards, and only very partially revealed the lower section, with its rugged discoloured surfaces, pitted and gnarled, and presenting everywhere a most forbidding appearance. Presently, as the eyes of our adventurers became more accustomed to the gloom, what was an evident ship's lantern was observed swinging overhead, for the opening of the long-closed door in the trunk had induced a strong upward draught, indicative of openings above, and at first the object had struck Harold at least with a thrill of horror, so closely did it resemble a weird head suspended in the surrounding gloom. Crossing and recrossing from side to side, and having, so far as could yet be seen, small platforms by way of landings, there went upwards a kind of half stairs, half ladder, made of rattan, and evidently wound together with great care, and giving ready access to the upper portion of the mysterious tree.

"Just as he described it," muttered Dubec; and then he showed his companion that the door, or valve, at the foot of this strange staircase was furnished with an iron bar, made to fit into iron sockets let into the thickness of the hollow trunk on each side, for the door itself was not one-third of the thickness of the hollow trunk, and, being flush outside, left, when closed, a deep recess inside.

While these observations were making, Harold noticed that the wind was rising, and drew his companion's attention to the fact that some of the red ashes of their fire, which was still burning, were blowing in at their feet, and, dreading the effect of this on the inflammable rattans of the staircase, they shouldered to the door, which worked reluctantly on its huge wooden pivots.

"Now," said Dubec, "we have only to go up and help ourselves. It is very simple, is it not?"

"What is simple?" asked Harold, on whom an undefined, but unnerving, horror was slowly advancing, as he expressed it to himself, inch by inch.

Dubec only laughed a low, strange laugh, and replied, "Allez, go you the first, my friend;" and his companion, upon whom the weird interior of the tree had already produced a sort of nightmare, obeyed as in a dream, and slowly went up the rattan stairway, followed by the recidivist.

VII.—Finding the Treasure.

Harold, although by no means constitutionally a coward, such as civilisation and what may be conventionally called a carpet-and-pavement life now unduly fosters, was not brave in the positive sense, and, as he expressed it to himself inwardly, although not in those words, he went up the rattan stairs with the grave before him, or rather above him, and death behind, for somehow the idea had taken a firm hold of his excited fancy that Dubec, so soon as the treasure was actually found, had resolved on his murder.

A yard or two up, and he perceived overhead a close kind of ceiling of strong cane-work, and, cautiously exploring with his smoking, flickering torch, found himself half way through a kind of hatchway which opened on a sort of chamber, pierced by another turn of the rude but convenient rattan stairs, and presently, stepping on the floor, which was of great strength, he looked about him to see what kind of a place it was. By degrees the fantastic and forbidding shadows yielded to his eyes, as they grew accustomed to the obscurity, and presently Dubec also emerged on the platform, and thus adding to the general illumination, the rough outline of the chamber became vaguely visible. It appeared to have been used as a kind of store. Casks and cases were built up against the sides, and in one angle was a stand of old-fashioned muskets, together with a number of swords, pikes, &c., and a small pile of kegs, which, as Dubec's eye fell on them, caused him to mutter "Gunpowder!" Harold could not help looking longingly at the arms, but somehow he felt himself constrained not to go near them, as he had an inward perception that his companion was eyeing him suspiciously, and he dreaded the moment when the old convict should throw off his clumsy mask, and declare that he had only been amusing him with the promise of sharing the spoil.

"Nothing here but the spiders, you see," observed Dubec, gruffly, and obviously all had been undisturbed for a long period, seeing that all around were thick festoons of cobwebs—not such as are ever seen in Europe, but webs capable of catching and holding fast any small bird.

"If the spiders are like the webs," observed Harold, breaking a strange silence that had fallen upon both, "they must be rather ugly customers."

"*Certainement*," replied Dubec, and, approaching his torch to one of the largest webs, he revealed to view a spider quite as large as a small crab, ensconced in his citadel, amid the *débris* of some recent meal off a terrible-looking form of beetle which had already filled Harold with a nameless horror.

Dubec did not offer to touch any of the articles in the chamber, and presently, turning to Harold, he said, "I see no sign of the treasure here. It is above—we must seek it," and to his companion's surprise and secret relief—for he shuddered to have the old convict behind him—slowly climbed up the second staircase.

Presently the two emerged on another floor of woven cane, and, as they simultaneously raised their torches, paused in silent astonishment as they gradually took in the details of the scene before them. It was a large apartment, with what appeared to be French windows of lattice work at one end, closed, and opening, as Harold conjectured, on some kind of platform extended on the branches of the tree, which he calculated began to run out at about this height. The walls were draped with flags, which he made out to be in many cases tattered and torn, and here and there a mirror shone, dim and unreflecting, amid the strange drapery—mirrors that had once been the adornment of some ship's saloon. Piles of soft cushions lay along the floor, and there were musical instruments, with heaps of music and books, and a number of small objects for use or ornament, whose exact character they could not immediately discern. Up in one corner, nearest to the square hatch in the floor where the rattan stairs ended, was a kind of alcove, and to this the eyes of both turned and rested there, fixed for the moment by an overpowering fascination.

"Yes, yes," muttered Dubec, in a voice so subdued that Harold drew nearer to distinguish his words; "Philippe was true. It is all as he said. See, my friend, this is the bridal chamber, as he called it. Outside" (pointing to the lattice-work windows) "was their general apartment, right out on the tree—a kind of balcony, where, he told me, they used to hang up festoons of flowers and gaily-coloured birds, and sing and play together. Here is the treasure, my friend, unless reptiles can digest diamonds, and spiders can swallow sapphires."

On a low kind of reclining chair, at the foot of the alcove, was a dark oblong object, which Harold now took up, an action that made Dubec turn sharply, and ask, "What is that?"

"Only a kind of old-fashioned prayer-book, so far as I can see," replied Harold, holding out what was in truth an ancient breviary, of great weight, richly embellished and ponderously clasped.

"Now," said Dubec, drawing still nearer, first twisting his torch into a chair back, and plunging one hand into the bosom of his torn shirt, as though to feel for something there, "here we have bed and bier in one. See! the glorious tricolour, the conquering flag of Philippe's ship, covers the corpse and the treasure too. Look!" And, twitching the corner of a large tricoloured flag that lay like a counterpane on an unmistakable bed, he motioned Harold to approach with his torch. The latter obeyed him, moving as one in a dream, and still mechanically holding the breviary in his right hand. He approached, raised the smoking torch so as to cast the light downwards, and saw, amid a terrible glitter of red and white gems, a sight that seemed to him, overwrought as his nerves were, so horrible in its living corruption that he started back, wildly exclaiming, "My God! my God, I cannot bear it! I cannot bear it!"

"Fool!" Dubec stamped his foot angrily. "Do you think I brought you here for nothing. Fool, they are only reptiles. Quick, pick me out the stones instantly, I say. Do you hear? It is my fancy, my will that you do this. Do you understand? You are an Englishman, and only fit for such dirty work as this. Quick, I say, or ——," and he drew forth his hand from his bosom and levelled the pistol that had already done such execution among the Queensland blacks point blank at Harold. For him there was no time for thought. Apart from the peril that thus suddenly faced him, he had turned to fly as far as possible from that indescribably horrible and revolting sight, and in a blind, unreasoning impulse had started to dash through the windows, regardless of what lay beyond, or whither he was going, but as he turned, he threw, more by a blind instinct than design, the heavily-bound breviary at Dubec. It struck with full force the hand that held the pistol, and, despite the iron muscles of the old recidivist, beat his hand down, and, as the muzzle pointed to the rattan floor, the charge exploded just as Harold sprang right through the old and decayed lattice, and, carried on by his impetus, fell sprawling on the platform that extended far out, built solidly on the horizontal boughs of the giant tree.

Then—as he lay prostrate, bruised, and half stunned—a roar as of a thousand cannon seemed to rend the air, and a lightning flash of awful red fire revealed each crack and grain of dust on the platform on which he rested, and the whole mighty mass of timber rocked to and fro like the mast of a storm-tossed ship.

"Oh, my God!" he whispered, for his voice seemed to have gone for the moment under the paralysing influence of the awful shock. "The gunpowder—he has blown up the magazine!" While he lay still he heard the unmistakable crackling of wood and the dull roar of fire, as when a strong furnace is in full blast, and he knew that the tree was on fire!

Staggering up, like a drunken man, he retraced his steps to the windows or door, through which he had burst just in time to save himself from the effects of the explosion, and there the sight he saw warned him that by the way he and his companion had come there was no passage now for anything in the shape of flesh and blood. All before him was thick smoke, with that peculiar odour that always accompanies gunpowder explosions on a large scale, and this smoke was irradiated with a fearful red glow.

The heat was intense, and evidently the fire was rapidly gaining a hold of the tree, and Harold tottered back, half blinded, to the external platform, and then grew conscious of what had previously escaped his attention. The terrible roar and hissing of the fire within was now answered by an increasing roar without—a growl, a rattle, a scream ever and anon, but of hurricane magnitude, while splashes of tempest water, the mere drops of the growing tropical storm, began beating in on the platform on which he now lay clinging to the uneven surface, for even in this comparative shelter the wind was blowing with a mighty power, and he had not strength to stand up against it.

All beyond his lofty station was not simply dark, but solidly black, as it seemed to his straining eyes, and in his awful solitude, thus strangely imprisoned on this giddy platform, between fire and tempest, he felt his brain reel and his heart stand still, as a dreadful deadening presentiment came over him that now, indeed, he was lost! Then, while the choking smoke rolled out on the platform, and the ominous hiss and seething of the fire sounded each moment nearer, the solid darkness which he dared not look at direct as he lay face downward on the platform, now running with water like a wave-washed deck—the solid darkness, I say, was not so much rent and split up as replaced by the most terrible blaze of tropical lightning, followed by the crash around of falling timber and then by a downpour of water as though an aërial lake were being poured down upon the forest. Even lying thus comparatively sheltered, for there were mighty branches far over Harold's head, he felt as though he should suffocate, so fierce was the swirl of the hurricane, and an apathy stole over him—a deadness to all feeling—against which he did not even struggle, and a merciful unconsciousness came to his rescue.

How long this swoon lasted Harold could never rightly tell. Perhaps it was right through the night and succeeding day, and the following night too, but suddenly he found himself conscious, and, greatly to his own astonishment, alive. The platform, on which he still lay, was quite dry, the air was distinctly warm and balmy with a thousand sweet and fresh scents, such as always succeed one of these tremendous tropical storms; the golden sunlight was glancing through the foliage that partly curtained the platform, and against a patch of bright sky that came within his vision were two or three birds of paradise lazily floating on their indescribably beautiful plumage.

All was still and peaceful, and it seemed to him as a dream from which he feared to awaken. But the sight of the platform on which he lay recalled his scattered senses, and, rising, he looked about him and gradually managed to realise all that had happened. He felt himself a changed man—weak from all he had gone through, and sick for want of nourishment, he yet experienced a strength unknown before, for his preservation so far appeared to him little less than miraculous. Proceeding with caution, he again entered the tree—for there was now no sign of fire—and gradually took in a view of what had been the extent of the catastrophe which had apparently overwhelmed the treasure-seeker and the treasure itself in a common ruin.

Terrible, indeed, had been the ruin and havoc wrought by the explosion and subsequent fire. The whole interior was charred black, and here and there heaps of ashes, or in some instances fantastically-shaped masses of cinder, showed where the fittings and appointments of the upper chamber had once been. The alcove itself was gone entirely. It had probably been deeply hollowed out of the thickness of the comparative shell to which the tree had been reduced, and the force of the explosion had torn it out, leaving a great jagged gap. This had evidently materially aided in putting out the fire, as the sheets of tropical rain had been blown in, and Harold noticed that much of the ash was turned into a kind of horrible slush, in which he shuddered to tread. The whole force of the gunpowder seemed to have been spent in an upward and a lateral direction, and happily, from some unexplained cause, the principal stress of the concussion had been exhausted on the very corner where Dubec had stood almost overshadowing the glittering treasure he was doomed to see, but not to touch! The whole of the firmly woven floor here was gone, and, looking down in the black gulf below, it became pretty evident that most of the stairway was destroyed too, and so far as could be seen the cavity was filled up to a great extent with the water-soaked *débris* of the fire. Strange as it may appear, Harold felt no pang at the loss of the treasure. A sense of unspeakable relief had come over him. He did not in so many words rejoice at the catastrophe that had swept his companion out of existence, but he experienced an all-pervading sense of freedom from something that had been really as loathsome to him as was the hideous sight he had seen just for an instant under the mocking canopy of the victorious tricolour.

His first impulse was to get out of the tree, which was to him a thing accursed; and, cautiously feeling his way, he found it practicable to scramble down to the lower chamber, where had been stored the magazine which, fired by the shot from Dubec's pistol, had precipitated the catastrophe. The tearing effect of the explosion had left here and there great gaps in the sides of the hollow part of the gigantic tree, and these facilitated descent, but, while on a projecting fragment of what had formed the platform of the store chamber, Harold began to consider whether he did not run a terrible risk of being precipitated to the bottom of what was now a well of soddened rubbish, and finding it impracticable, when once there, to open the valve which he well remembered he and Dubec had shouldered to on entering the tree. This mode of exit, however, was obviously the best, and he resolved to risk it, trusting to his agility to clamber up again in the event of an unforeseen difficulty, and, slowly feeling his way, he gradually lowered himself. This portion of the interior was by no means in thick darkness, for the shock that the tree had sustained had opened several rents in the trunk, through which shot a few ghostly arrows of fitful light, and at the worst Harold fancied he might enlarge some of the lower of these if emergency arose.

Much as Dubec had revolted him, he now began to feel, by a strange perversity, the loss of his companion, and, working his way in this sinister gloom, and amid the slimy *débris* of the explosion, he experienced an indescribable longing for that human companionship that was now utterly beyond his reach.

Suddenly it glanced across his mind that the treasure, after all, was not destroyed. Precious stones, he knew, might be resolved to vapour in a properly constructed furnace or crucible, but the fire in the tree had probably not raged long before it was extinguished by the fearful tropical rain; and then, had he not seen that a great part of the tree forming the wall of the alcove had been blown bodily out? Clearly, it was worth while to make a thorough search among the *débris* of the fire, and particularly of the glade round the tree; and, burning with a newborn eagerness to extricate himself, he redoubled his efforts, for he clearly recognised the need in which he stood to obtain some food, and to procure any he must first extricate himself from the tree. Shaking off his weakness Harold worked his way to the bottom of the shaft, which was not nearly so full as he had anticipated, and having in his groping come across some ship's cutlasses, which had been hurled down by the explosion from the upper wall around which they had been placed, he soon discovered, and, to his great joy, succeeded in prising back the secret door in the trunk, and admitted the cheering light of noon into the space below, which was strewn with a heterogeneous collection of articles and utensils hurled from their place in the store chamber by the force of the explosion. Once outside the tree he breathed more freely, and, before proceeding further, quenched his thirst at a small pool among many miniature lakes formed by the late tempest, and then sought for some taro root. He then rested, while surveying the ground around the base of the tree, and perceiving at a glance that it was covered with ashes, cinders and a variety of objects all more or less bearing the marks of fire, this reminded him of a new difficulty. He had no means of kindling the smallest spark, and must eat his meat, could he procure it, raw! He had heard, indeed, of the way in which fire is kindled by the friction of two dry sticks, but he doubted his ability to produce it thus, and at present all the wood about him was too damp or too full of the living sap for such an experiment to have the slightest chance of succeeding. Having satisfied, or rather stifled, the cravings of his stomach on some of the taro root and some fruit which he feared might prove poisonous, he set to work to make a thorough search of the *débris* and ashes and remains generally of the explosion and fire. He had a method, too, and marked out the ground in segments of a great circle, struck from the tree as a centre, and began a systematic search of one of these at once. To his utter astonishment he was at once rewarded by finding several of the precious stones that had shone out to him from the awful spectacle of the funereal couch under the canopy of the flag of France, and, after pursuing a patient search as long nearly as the light lasted, he found he had collected his hands full three or four times over of white and red stones, which he hoped might prove to be the diamonds and sapphires of which Dubec had spoken. The following day he continued his search but found no more, and, after some subsequently fruitless trials, he decided to seek the boat, and if possible get to sea, where he might make for some inhabited land, or perhaps be picked up by a passing vessel. Somehow, after carefully washing and re-examining the stones that had thus strangely fallen into his possession, Harold felt within himself certain that they were genuine gems, and the mere feeling of this seemed to give him new life, and to put a strength and nerve into him which he had hitherto been a stranger. It is a grand thing, no doubt, to hold a fortune in the hollow of your hand, and undoubtedly to our hero this handling of portable property was a sure means for imparting an energy to his mind, as well as a strength to his body, he had never known before.

In a day or two he felt himself sufficiently reinvigorated to seek out the place where the boat had been laid up, and found it exactly as it had been left; but the recent storm had converted the formerly shallow stream into a swift-flowing river, and Harold had no difficulty in dropping down to the bay into which it discharged itself. Here, indeed, he stayed awhile, collecting such necessaries as he could find by way of provisioning his little barque for a coasting voyage, and in due course managed, with infinite pains, to get out of the many cross currents created by the reefs in this part of the New Guinea coast, and then decided to stretch in an easterly course, as being, he thought, more likely to bring him in the track of some merchant ship, or possibly, of some mail steamer.

Harold was now, indeed, fortune favoured. He had not been beyond the perilous "white water" of the reefs that lie off North-West New Guinea many hours before his little craft was sighted and picked up by a Dutch merchantman bound for Amsterdam. As matters turned out, it was no great loss to him that he had to communicate by signs. He was taken for a shipwrecked waif, and kindly treated, and he had enough leisure to mature his plan for getting his gems valued. He produced one or two of the stones and traded them with the captain, who, he soon found, knew them to be genuine; and, having thus obtained a change of clothes and a few necessaries, on his arrival at Amsterdam he set to work to dispose of part of his stock of precious stones. He knew all along that he was being terribly imposed upon, but even at that disadvantage, he realised a very considerable sum indeed by the sale of Philippe's diamonds, which represented, by the way, the concentrated proceeds of much piracy on British commerce. He sent no letter to herald his arrival in England as a man of independence, but it was not long before he married the object of his boyhood's fancy. He sent out to inquire how much Mr. Walcot had lost through the exchange of coats, and in due course made the amount good, with interest. He says that he cannot be too grateful to Providence, and that, as he looks back and sees the way in which his course of life, so far, has been mapped out, he is lost in wonder at the good fortune that has been showered on him, and both he and his wife are resolved to make really good use of the wealth that has come to them out of the pirates' hoards. Truth is stranger than fiction, and in this story of the Treasure we have one more illustration of the well-worn saying. Not only has Harold, as he says, brought the gold for a wedding ring from the Austral world, but he has had three of the very finest diamonds set in a ring for Norma, which she declares is a great deal too splendid to wear, although I believe she does wear it pretty often; while Harold tells her that, after all, it is not the sapphires and the diamonds, rich as they were, but his wife that has proved the true Treasure of the Tree to which the old convict so strangely led him.

A MAD PASSION.

I.—The Prologue.

We had done well that season. There was no doubt about it, and my wife, who was rather of the pessimist type, now admitted as much. Our farm lay snugly nestled in a valley on a winding stream that ran, when there was any water, into the Clarence, and we as emigrants from dear old Devonshire had done our utmost to plan everything as much like a typical farm there as possible. I had several hired labourers, who swore my service was better than independence, as well the rascals might, seeing that I had nearly ruined myself during two fearful droughts by maintaining them in comparative idleness; and we had a charming dwelling-house on the top of a swelling green eminence rising out of a scooped-out hollow among surrounding hills, for all the world, as my homely-speaking and homely-thinking wife declared, like a cup and saucer, only the cup was very small and the saucer exceedingly large. I say my wife was homely, but that is only in a domestic sense. She was essentially a lady by birth, breeding, and education, and although one of my own ancestors has a representative in a bust of a distinguished worthy in the Valhalla of the West of England, the Taunton Town Hall, and although I had a thorough old-fashioned English education at Cheltenham, I often feel my inferiority to my wife intellectually, for homely as she was domestically, she has another side to her character, and when the Bishop of Sydney paid us a visit not long ago, she received more than one evidently spontaneous compliment from his Grace as to the way in which she had trained up her son—our only child —who is now a most promising scholar in a Sydney collegiate school, whither we have sent him at a great personal sacrifice, feeling that he cannot receive the right kind of training here. Although quite a child in years he is very precocious and exceedingly well-informed generally for his age, and it seems that when the good bishop visited the college he was much struck by our lad, who had signalised himself by his altogether remarkable knowledge of Scripture, which is decidedly the work of his mother before we, with suppressed tears, sent him from us to the metropolis of the colony. But this is all very discursive. I, Andrew Chambers, came out some fourteen years ago to try farming in the parent colony, and, up to the present—barring droughts and some trifling troubles—have had nothing but good fortune, until last year, when something happened to us which unfortunately has been grossly perverted by a scurrilous newspaper in want of a sensation, and as I am determined that no shadow of calumny shall rest on our good name for the sake of our boy, I have determined to set down, in the most plain and matter of fact manner, the story of the terrible incident that happened to us some two years since, and which has been raked up from the ashes of the dead, and utterly perverted, because it pleased me to offer myself as a candidate for a seat in the Assembly, and my political opponents resorted to the weaving of a most abominable tissue of libels to damage my moral character with the electorate. Further, what happened to me and furnished the unfortunate foundation for a tissue of malicious reports, seems to me a thing that might well, in the wonderful coincidences of life, happen to any other settler so situated, and may indeed have done so for aught I know. Thus much by way of preface, and now for my story.

II.—My Story Begins.

About two years ago or so, when we were first beginning to prosper and had sent our boy away to Sydney, my wife fell into a bad state of health. She had over-exerted herself, and I was so much engaged with my sheep and crops that I had not noticed the fact as I ought to have done, until at last her evident illness was forced upon my notice. It happened that the wife of one of my men had been called in to act as house servant, but somehow my wife could not bear her. She was a great, strong woman, who wore boots like a navvy's, and slapped everything down, and not only spoke out at the top of her voice, but laughed out and joined in our conversation when we sat down to dinner. This sort of thing was particularly offensive to my wife, and indeed to me, only I was more generally absorbed in some kind of all-engrossing business and did not notice. One day my wife said, "I really think, dear, we might now afford a servant. I mean one of those sent out specially for domestic service. I do not feel so strong as I used, and it would be a great comfort, I think, for us to have a nice, quiet young girl in the house. Besides, if you think of having those Sydney people here I never could bear to have that fearful, clattering cart-horse of a woman to wait at table, and you would be laughed at as a regular rustic, or a wild man of the Back Blocks."

When I went forth after the conversation just recorded to my usual pastoral and agricultural duties —for I raised both wool and corn, and had even a bit of a vineyard too—I could not somehow get the subject of the proposed servant out of my head. I had readily consented that we should endeavour to obtain one from Sydney, and my wife was to write to a trusted and familiar friend there to look out for a suitable person. I may here remark that Margaret, my wife, was colonial born. I took up my allotment promptly on arriving, sinking in it nearly all my available capital. After just six months of the utter loneliness of a bachelor life as a settler I felt I should go mad, and determined to find a wife somehow. It is a habit of the Australian settler to locate himself as far as practicable from his neighbour, instead of uniting to form one great village community, as they tell me is the case in Russia, and I went up to Sydney, to look after some agricultural implements, resolved to find a partner if I could. Six months among the sheep had been all too much for me. I did not mind the day, for I worked hard, but the night! Someone has said that solitude is one of the highest enjoyments of which our souls are susceptible. I cannot say it is to me. I rather fancy that those persons are fitter for solitude who are like nobody else and who are not liked by anybody.

Anyway, I fell in with my Margaret, and somehow, greatly to the surprise of her family, we made up our minds to get married. Margaret was not happy at home, for she had an intemperate brother, and she was glad, she said, to exchange the town for the country, and I, too, was certainly glad to have her.

And now I must confess that I had innocently practised one deception on my part which, slight as it was, or as it seemed to me at the time, was nearly fatal to us in a way as terrible as it was unforeseen.

The facts, for this is the place to give them, are brief and simple. Prior to emigrating, I had as a youth—at that indeterminate period when one is neither man nor boy—been sent to a clever "coach" at Cheltenham—a place much affected by colonists and tutors—and I was to be fitted for the army. I was not studious, but fond of outdoor life, and I had, they said, no application; and, anyway, I know I did not learn anything. In the issue my father, disgusted at my repeated failures, sent me out to New South Wales with the little capital that was to have been mine to eke out my pay as a subaltern had I qualified for Her Majesty's service. Well, there is nothing very particular here, is there? I never was used to the pen, so my awkwardness must be excused; but, nevertheless, there is very much in it, for while at Cheltenham I had the misfortune to contract an attachment with a girl that I can never think of without a shudder, and I am not by any means naturally nervous. She was a bold, finely-grown, and utterly precocious child of about fifteen, and, as I conceived, of marvellous physical beauty. In truth, there is no use in decrying her personal attractions; they were many and real, and quite turned my impressionable and giddy boy's head. She was the daughter of our laundress, and came with the washing, and that is how I first saw her. I and the other lads at the tutor's had far too much liberty, and Alice and I contrived to meet. I was full of all manner of fine projects, and she was, as I know now, only too anxious to entangle a simple-minded boy who was supposed to have excellent prospects. I even went into letter writing, and copied very silly verses in her praise, and was such a young idiot as to address her as "wifie," and other nonsense of the kind. Ay, it is grave enough when I think of it all, and my story should be a warning to all young fellows who fancy the first pretty girl who crosses their path. In reality, on my side the whole affair was perfectly innocent, only I shudder to think how near the abyss I was once or twice when the artful, wily creature affected a more than usual abandonment to her feelings, and thus quickened mine into an enthusiasm as perilous as it was pure, for all the time Alice was acting a part. In the end I made such a mess of my studies that my father descended on the scene and packed me off as a parcel of bad goods to Sydney—a thing fathers in England do much too often, considering the fact that such ne'er-do-wells as are thus expatriated usually go from bad to worse, and finally help to swell a mass of misery and vice which but for them would hardly exist.

It happened that I went out to Sydney in a sailing ship, partly for economy to husband my little capital and partly for health's sake, as I was supposed to have developed a consumptive tendency, which turned out to be a doctor's fallacy. The captain was Cornish born, of some sixty years. He was a temperance man, very seriously minded, and disposed to play the father to all on board. He took much notice of me, and somehow won my confidence, and gave me much excellent advice. Somehow he elicited the stupid story of my enthusiastic attachment to the laundress's daughter at Cheltenham, and advised me when I reached what he called a new world to determine to begin all afresh. "Forget everything of the past, and treat it as it had never been at all," he urged. "Make up your mind to work hard; nothing is so moral, my lad, as downright hard manual work. Go up country and stick to the soil; if I hadn't the good ship *Hesperus*, I should have a farm, I can tell you; the sea or the field—that is my motto. Look out for some sensible girl—Australian born, mind you—and get married early; that makes a man steady. You know what Robbie Burns tells us—

>   To mak' a happy fireside clime
>   For weans and wife,
>   Is the true pathos and sublime
>   Of human life.

And mind you, if you are wise, say nothing about your first attachment, your calf love. Let all be fresh and straight; feel that you have been born anew, as it were, and you'll get on, never fear."

There was a good deal more that the honest old boy told me, but this was the pith thereof, and when I settled down on my allotment near the Clarence, I felt that I was realising the fruits of good advice, and when I saw my Margaret and she consented to abandon Sydney and go up with me into rural loneliness, I was, as they say, in the seventh heaven. I not only never breathed a word to Maggie, as I delighted to call her, of my Cheltenham love affair, but I practically forgot all about it—as far as anyone can forget such an episode. It became to me, indeed, quite a vague reminiscence and as a thing that had happened to someone else, and—I do not pretend to any metaphysics or psychology, as I believe the fine writers call it, but to my plain common sense it did seem to have happened to someone else. I did not feel like the creature I had been in England, and when my wife archly asked me if I had never spoken to any other girl as I spoke to her, I could, with a clear conscience exclaim, "Never!" I did not mean a bit to be what is called Jesuitical; I meant it, and I now affirm that it was the truth. I may have used some of the *words*, but as for the *feeling*—why, who would dream of comparing a silly boy's fancied love to the intense, utterly true, and passionate affection of a man who cleaves to his wife with all the force implied in the Bible phrase?

Still, I now admit it had been better infinitely had I told my wife about Alice, only I could not endure the idea of responding to all the curious enquiries that would have resulted thence. My wife had a pretty way of self-depreciation and calling herself " plain," and sometimes " an ugly thing," and I did not like the idea of her asking was Alice pretty. And had she done so, somehow, say what I might, I felt she would have drawn me into confessing that Alice *was* not only pretty but beautiful, and altogether I preferred to act on the counsel of my Cornish friend and drop a veil over my past and youthful folly.

I *knew* that I loved my wife utterly with an undivided heart; why, then, rake up all the rubbish of my silly idle youth?

Still I now admit that I was wrong; but then how could I possibly foresee what was in store for us?

And now to my narrative. I was specially busy with my agricultural and pastoral work, and also deeply engaged in some experimental vine dressing, when one evening my wife informed me that her Sydney friend had found us a servant. "And," she went on, "I understand, such a treasure! Helen writes: 'I am sure you will approve of my choice, and if I had not engaged the girl she would have been snapped up fifty times over. She is very nice, and quite refined, and yet *so* domesticated. She is ready to do everything you want. When I read out your little list, she said to each item, " Oh, certainly, I should be quite willing to do *that*," and she seemed anxious to get into "the Bush," and she appears to me to be a very modest, well-meaning young woman, only '——"

"Only what?' I asked, for my wife stopped, evidently

reluctant to read further, but now my curiosity was roused, and men are quite as curious as women sometimes, and I repeated my question.

"Oh, nothing," replied my wife, folding up the letter and putting it in her pocket. "Helen thinks that the girl is too much of a lady in appearance, but if she is really willing to do what we want, why should *we* mind?"

"What is her name?" I enquired, a strange feeling suddenly coming over me, for which I could in no way account.

"Elizabeth Carter; she is coming down with those things you are expecting, and is to be here at the end of the week."

Elizabeth Carter. Something within me said "Thank God!" for in an instant an awful terror—I can use no other word—had seized me, strong man as I am admitted to be, and I felt as though some dreadful calamity had been within a hair's-breadth of descending on our house, like a destroying avalanche.

III.—My Wife Brightens up.

My experiments with the vines had come to a successful crisis, and my shepherds gave me the most encouraging reports of my approaching "clip." I had noticed my wife's dulness and a worn look about her eyes and a drooping of the figure, and I resolved, directly I had reached a certain point of prosperity, to take her to Sydney, where she could be better amused; I also thought that we might have our boy home then and let him go to a day college.

I mentioned my future plans to Maggie, and was delighted to perceive that she brightened much, and I said, playfully, "You see, my dear, you were not designed to blossom in the wilderness after all, and yearn back to the pavement and the shops, and the city gas lamps."

"It is quite true," she replied; "but you cannot imagine, with all your work, during a long day, what it is to be here in this large house almost alone, and you know how seldom anyone calls to stay. If this girl is good for anything I mean to set up some dairy work and find an occupation there. I cannot bear doing things alone. I don't think you would like to work without your men and horses, and even the shepherds have their sheep, you know. The truth is, I miss the child dreadfully, and I would have him back to-morrow if it were not such a cruel, selfish thing to do."

That was so like my good, dear, unselfish wife. I took her in my arms on a sudden impulse and kissed her again and again.

IV.—The New Maid.

DURING the next few days the coming of Elizabeth Carter entirely escaped my mind. I had very much to make me extremely anxious. All along I had been ambitious and had toiled patiently in pursuit of an end which now seemed coming into full view. In a word, I was looking for comparative emancipation from my lonely and isolated position, and I began to dream dreams of a course of social enjoyment, wherewith I longed to reward my dear, uncomplaining wife for all her self-denial and for all the terribly solitary hours she had to pass during my long absences from home.

It is curious, but true, that the first near approach of supreme success, or what a man deems to be such, is harder to bear than the deferred hope and the toil and burden of working to achieve that success. I found myself growing very nervous indeed, as I perceived signs, unmistakable to me, that in all probability I should soon be one more of the fortunate colonists who find themselves suddenly wealthy men. I nursed all this secretly, as I became more and more convinced of the fact that this great change was nearing us. I became more reserved, and, indeed, I had need of reserve to keep down my inward excitement, and the more as I determined not to tantalise my wife with surmises and mere anticipations, but to wait until our fortune should be really assured. No doubt this was, after all, a piece of personal, and perhaps selfish, eccentricity, but, anyhow, I persisted in it, and consequently presented just at this time, I fear, rather a sullen front to my wife than otherwise.

One evening I came in thoroughly exhausted, in a physical sense, for I had been far under a blistering sun, and had been nearly blinded by a dust storm.

Our house was a flat, like most bush residences, and the room where we usually sat and had our meals was next to the kitchen, while opposite was a small affair, a sort of office, devoted to me alone, where I had put up a rude desk, a stool, a home-made ricketty tripod and a number of shelves, and where I had samples of wool, glass jars containing different varieties of wheat berries and some filled with flours, and here I worked at my accounts and attended to my correspondence against the calling of the mailman, calculated my wages and how my stores of rations stood, and generally transacted my business. My wife never came in here; she said the place smelled of grease and dust, and often rallied me on bringing the smell away with me. There was a second door from this sanctum opening on an enclosure behind, where agricultural utensils were stored. The bedrooms —we had three—lay back, and around the front of the building was the usual verandah.

I say I was tired, and, sinking into a low wicker-work arm-chair, I rested, uttering only one word, "Tea." I was too weary even to light a pipe or a cigar, a thing generally reserved for the quiet evening, and there I sat, half dozing, utterly tired, drinking tea, until at last my wife remarked: "You don't say what you think of her?" "Think of her?" I repeated. "What her?" "Why, the new maid, to be sure! Anybody would think we had always been waited on. But it is like you, to be sure; when I have only one earring on, it's all the same to you. However, the girl has come. She brought in the things just now. You must be blind indeed not to have seen her."

"Well, I was nearly blinded to-day by the dust, but really, Maggie, I never saw anyone but you. She must have a very noiseless footfall."

"I never thought of that," was the meditative rejoinder. "Now you mention it, I suppose she is very still, but she seems quick and willing, and perhaps she may suit us. I am sure I want some fellow-creature here."

I roused myself a little, inwardly chafed to think that my wife should be thrown on such a resource, but I made no remark, saying inwardly, "It will not be for long." "Well," my wife went on, "you seem very glum indeed to-night. Have all the sheep strayed away into Victoria?"

"My dear, I am not 'glum,' only exhausted; that's all. I have taken too much out of myself to-day, and now am good for nothing."

"I really don't know," she replied, getting out her work basket, "what's the use of your toiling so hard. Since we sent the child away I know the house has been inexpressibly wretched, and now that we have this girl, what are we to do with her? She can't sit all alone by herself. I know what that is like, and I suppose we can't have her in here" (this said tentatively) "to help me with this needlework."

"You can have her in if you like" was my answer, for, refreshed by my tea and rest, I recollected that some work was awaiting me in my office, and now that the fit was on me for work, I was glad of the excuse to be alone. Somehow, such was the excitement into which I had lately drifted, that I felt I must go straight on to the end, and then—well then, if all turned out right, I intended to bid a long farewell to all kind of business.

When I came out of my office I found the room empty; wife and servant had evidently gone to bed. I thought now that I would have a cigar before turning in too, and accordingly lighted one. Somehow it would not "draw," and I looked about for a long pin. My wife had left her workbox open, and I sought there for a pin, and in doing so came on the letter from our Sydney friend which she had only partially read out to me. Some curious feeling prompted me to take it up, and my eyes fell on the passage omitted in reading out the letter aloud. The words were "only she is almost too good-looking; but I know your husband is not like some of whom we have heard, so I don't think it really matters."

My wife was asleep when I joined her, and as I had to be a great way off by the following noon, I rose before she did, breakfasted on bread and milk, and was away before the new maid was visible.

V.—" I find you Married a Hard, Cold, Stone-like Man."

That day I found myself on my way back in a much more pleasant frame of mind. There had been no dust storm, and all had gone well; and as I cantered back alone the remembrance of the previous day came back, conveying the unpleasant conviction that I had been at the best a very bearish kind of husband. "What a pity," I said to myself, "that at such times our wives cannot see within us, looking through and through us, and thus discriminating between appearance and reality!"

All along on one side, as I went thus communing with myself, was a vast line of flame trees, looking for all the world like a forest of deep pink and crimson flames, smokeless and stationary, for there was no wind, and these vividly coloured masses of gigantic blossomings struck even me as singularly impressive. As I rode on past some beautiful spots I caught now and then the note of a far-away bell or lyre bird. It is a very strange note, not heard, I believe, anywhere out of the Austral hemisphere, and resembles a soft bell gently tolling forth low-voiced aërial chimes. The whole scene was lovely and soft, and with the stillness and beauty thereof a kind of enervating voluptuousness seemed borne in on me while pausing to drink in the full effect of the lovely surroundings.

Throwing off the feeling which somehow seemed particularly unwelcome to my mood, I pushed on and soon entered a sort of gully full of fine fern trees, which led directly to my home.

The reins had dropped on the neck of my well-trained horse, who was breaking into a canter, anxious to get his evening feed and rest, when I suddenly caught up the bridle and pulled up short, for just in front there darted out from the fern fronds a woman—that was all I perceived at first—who cast out her arms and stumbled up against us. Instinctively I reached low to save her from falling, and, as the fire comes from the striking of the flint and steel, two words were uttered in a breath—"Andrew!" "Alice!" Then my presence of mind returned. I sprang down, drew my horse's bridle within my arm and looked at the woman before me, trying to trace out the form and features mirrored in the memory of a Past I had believed to be dead and buried beyond all resurrection here or hereafter. Something of the revulsion in my thoughts and look communicated itself to my unexpected companion. She drew aside a little, but was the first to speak, as I paused interrogatively.

"Yes, Elizabeth Carter, now your wife's servant. Do you remember that you vowed you would never forget me, that you would return some day or send for me? You have done neither, but I have come, and for the sake of my love I have humiliated myself. I am now at least near you—I shall see you—I shall have some comfort yet, before I pass away into oblivion."

I must own I was completely staggered by these words, and still more by the manner of the speaker. Was it acting—the artifice of a designing woman? Alas, no! I would it had been. There was something in the tone, much more than in the highflown words, that thrilled me with a dread such as I had never felt before, and such as I trust I shall never feel again. She went on: "You are silent. How changed you are! Do you remember how you urged me to 'improve' myself, to become educated, to seek to raise myself? Well, have I not done it? You shall soon judge. I have kept your promises before me all these years, and mine I am fulfilling. I have left all to follow and find you. I find you married—a hard, cold, stone-like man, and yet I have things you wrote, things you swore——"

"For God's sake!" I interrupted, "no more of this. Are you in your senses? I may have said and done foolish things when I was a boy, but what is that to me now? If you had any true womanly feeling, and if what you say is true, you would have avoided me of all men in the world.

Did I ever hold out hope or promise after our parting?"

"No! no!" she replied passionately, "but I resolved to be true, and, indeed, I could not help what has been done. I have tried to forget you, but I could not. Some power beyond my comprehension has drawn me to you, and now I am content. I am your servant, Andrew, and that at least is gain."

I paused to think. Was the poor girl mad? That was the question I asked myself seriously, or was she simply a wicked, designing woman? I would test this, any way. Summoning as much harshness as I could into my voice and manner I said, "All this is folly, and worse. Say 'our service does not suit you, return to Sydney and I will pay your way back to England and——" In my agitation, as I thought of my wife and all the fearful misconstruction that might be put on all this, I felt mad myself and ready to promise anything; but Alice, for so I will call her, drew herself up and burst forth in a passionate fit of sobbing, crying "Kill me! kill me! but don't, don't send me away!" I hate to narrate all this, but facts are facts, and after all, whatever may have been my folly as a boy, I have nothing to reproach myself with since, and it was only a feeling of common humanity that led me to mollify my tone and try to soothe the fearfully excited girl. All the time I kept the bridle of the horse tightly over my arm, for I felt that every moment she might cast herself in my arms. And, in one word, I did not know what to do, and was veritably at my wits' ends.

It is much too painful to give in detail the rest of that fearful meeting. Briefly the case stood thus: Alice appeared to have been solely drawn to join me in New South Wales by an ever-growing affection which she herself could not account for, she candidly admitted, declaring that my total silence had only made her more resolute to find me out before she died. She had preserved all my boyish effusions, and with a simplicity which gave me inexpressible pain, she quoted some tender passages which had been, she affirmed, her solace and lodestar, and she protested that she had no choice but to follow me to the end of the world. She indignantly repelled the insinuation that she had any base motive. No money, she affirmed, should buy my letters, and if we sent her away she would return and lie across our door, and, in a word, she went into a rhapsody of what was doubtless high-flown nonsense, but which all the same was inexpressibly shocking to me. I felt, as I have said, at my wits' end. What should, what could I do?

It is easy for those who read my story—dreadful even to narrate—to be wise and virtuous and say what I ought to have done, but things are very different at the time of their occurrence from what they appear when coldly related. Alice was in earnest and I felt full of unspeakable remorse for the foolish vows of my forgotten silly youth. I finally did what was doubtless wrong, but what seemed to me, face to face with her intense excitement and deep distress, essential—I temporised. I pacified her. She should not be sent off, at any rate then. We must see. She was foolish to feel as she did, and if she stayed on she would soon perceive that the Andrew of Cheltenham had no longer any existence. He had perished. I would befriend her, but she must not dare to speak to me again as she had done, nor indeed to approach me in any way. I was entirely devoted to my wife, and to no other woman in the world, and here I spoke proudly, because I knew I spoke truly. Let her get rid of all this hysteria. I would be a good master and my wife a good mistress, and so on; and before I had come within sight of home I persuaded her to leave me and to think over what I had said, and my last words were: "Remember, there is no more to me any Alice. I do not know her. Henceforth to me you are only Elizabeth Carter."

VI.—The Plot Deepens.

On that eventful evening my wife accorded me a warmer welcome than usual. The mailman had brought her a letter from our boy of which we were both exceedingly proud, seeing it was so well written and spelled. As a rule Maggie was far from demonstrative, but when she did go out of herself no one could be more ardent, and even impulsive, than she, and her eyes sparkled with eager delight when I told her that I was determined some way or other to have our boy again with us. It happened that evening that one or two of our neighbours, accompanied by their wives, rode over to visit us, and Elizabeth had as much as she could do to get tea and supper and help to make up two or three beds in our large spare room for those who stayed the night. These little interruptions to our monotonous, money-grubbing life, as Maggie frequently called it, did us both good. Husband and wife cannot well live alone together without grinding with more or less friction upon each other, and in the absence of any other society than their own, the smallest differences are sure to be magnified in a distorting atmosphere of self-assertion. Some of our guests were very nice people indeed, and I felt in wonderful spirits, the natural reaction after my trying experience of the afternoon, but I felt a twinge of pain when a squatter friend of ours, a man not given at any time to "trim" his conversation, burst out with "Where did you get that stunning pretty gal of yours?" while he gave great offence to my wife by adding that he had not seen such a kissable piece of goods for many a day, which rather coarse remark made his wife, who overheard it, give him a stinging box on the ear, which he laughed off, although it was no laughing matter. The fact is, some of us in this region were not particularly refined, and I believe the good lady of this particular squatter had, like her lord and master of many thousand sheep, risen from a very lowly estate across the great ocean.

That night, before sleeping, my wife spoke to me about Elizabeth. "I cannot quite make her out," she said; "the girl professes already to be very fond of me, and she certainly works well, but do you know, dear, she somehow makes me afraid of her. I cannot bear to come into contact with her, and then she is so dreadfully quiet and quick in all her movements. When we are not together, after you have gone off, I am always being surprised by her. She suddenly appears, as it were. I don't hear a sound, and yet, on turning my head, there she is!"

This was a new trait to me, and aroused some uneasy thoughts. I tried, however, to reassure my wife, and yet I felt within a strange fear that was all the worse to bear because it was quite vague.

Nothing occurred worthy of note for a while. Our guests went their various ways. Work was resumed as usual, and Elizabeth appeared to act perfectly well the part of a really good and attached maid as far as her mistress was concerned. To my inexpressible relief, she made not the smallest attempt to speak to me alone or in any way to revive the Alice of old. She seemed carefully to avoid meeting my eye, and I, for my own part, fully reciprocated this demeanour. 1 was much out of the house, and when in, took care never to enter the kitchen as I used to do when my wife reigned there as the only domestic deity. Still, although, so far, I had really nothing to complain of, my mind and conscience were ill at rest. I felt pity for Elizabeth, and an ever-increasing love for my wife; and it really seemed to me as though the advent of this girl, whom I was sometimes inclined to regard as deranged in mind—mad at all events on one point—had accentuated all my dormant affection for her mistress. The truth is, at a certain period in married life, if the husband is greatly engrossed in making his way, affection on his part is apt to become dormant and wholly undemonstrative. He is contented to repose on the recollection of long past endearments and transports, and thus forgets that his wife may be secretly starving for that very kind of heart-diet for which he has lost all present appetite.

I have said my mind and conscience were ill at rest.

Somehow I felt a daily increasing remorse at my own conduct. After all, said conscience, my conduct in compromising matters with Elizabeth had been cowardly and contemptible. Innocence has nought to fear. I had, after all, a secret understanding with a strange woman, introduced under our roof as a servant, and whatever might be the purity of my intentions I was so far wrong. The truth was I could not endure the thought of Maggie seeing any of the silly stuff I had once written to Alice, and I dreaded that, if defied, the girl would not hesitate in her mad passion to lay all these things before my wife. Surely my position was peculiarly cruel. Then, too, I had laid such stress to my wife on the fact that she was my first and only attachment, which was true enough in itself, and I had not, I suppose, the moral courage to confess that as a boy I had acted like a fool, and written letters, of the recollection of which I was heartily ashamed.

The question that most occupied me was how to extricate myself safely from this, to me, horrible mess.

VII.—I have an Idea.

At last an idea came to me. Directly my circumstances allowed, I would realise, and remove with my wife to Sydney and live there in a boarding-house or at an hotel. This surely would cut off the connection with Elizabeth Carter. I made up my mind to place a sum of money to her credit, and if she evinced any further disposition to plague me, why we would take our boy and go on a voyage somewhere. I could certainly, I thought, manage so that she should not be in the ship. No doubt many will ridicule my weakness and fears. I do so myself now in a sense; but in these cases the rule of put yourself in a like position should always be observed, and to me the situation had become very serious. I had got into the way of brooding over it during my lonely rides out in the bush and my work generally out of doors, and it happened, unfortunately, that I had no healthy-minded friend to whom I could resort. I had to keep the trouble to myself, and, as is usual in all such cases, it soon multiplied and exaggerated itself a thousand-fold.

My wife now openly remarked on my uneven, uncertain, snappish temper, as she rightly called it. She declared that if to prosper was to be so disagreeable, it were better far not to prosper at all; and what was particularly galling, she now complained that I was "a regular bear to Elizabeth." It was quite true. When Elizabeth said "good morning" or "good night," I did not take the smallest notice; and yet the formula went on all the same, and to me the iteration thereof was at times simply maddening. Sometimes, indeed, I would laugh out apparently at nothing, greatly to Maggie's astonishment, who could divine nothing of the cause; but I laughed in irony at the idea of my wife admonishing me for behaving like a bear to Elizabeth, the *servant*. Had she only known!

Then, again, another disappointment seized me in its grip. My wife now began preaching to me the advantages of simplicity and contentment. I had been blowing a cloud in my low American arm-chair and expatiating on all the fine things that I thought we might do by-and-by when the next "clip" was over, and supposing wool went up. Indeed, I could not help breaking out into lyrical gladness at thinking of what *that* might mean, and rather astonished Maggie by shouting out Garnet Walch's well-known lines:

> Fortune, ah! I have thee holden
> In what Scotia calls a " grup,"
> All my fleeces now are golden,
> Full Troy weight—for wool is up!

"I think, Andrew," she said, but in her kindest tones, "that you have been a little beside yourself of late. God knows, were it not for our boy I should ask nothing beyond what we have. Have you forgotten, dear, what you used to quote out of Ruskin when we first came into this wilderness—where he says that all true and wholesome enjoyments possible to mankind (I forget the exact words) have been just as possible since the earth was first made as now, and how he tells us that these true enjoyments are chiefly possible in peace? Do you not remember how he says that to watch the corn grow and the blossom set, to read, to think, to love, to hope—these are the things that have power to make us happy? Ah, there was one phrase I had forgotten—he adds, to pray. I am sure we ought to pray not to be tempted by the vanity of wealth if ever we come to it."

VIII.—A Strange Form of Love Letter.

A WISE English essayist has told us that *motive* is a sign of moral weakness, for he remarks *angels, i.e.*, presumedly perfectly good and pure beings, act on *impulse* only. I have thought of and applied this to my own case. On impulse I ought to have told my wife the whole story and thus defied Elizabeth Carter at the outset, but owing to my vacillation over the matter I now fell deeper and deeper into the inherent difficulties of the abnormal situation wherein I was now placed, and much as I longed to confess all to Maggie I found the task grow more impossible, as it seemed to me, every day.

A new fear now seized me. I found in the mornings, placed ostentatiously on my desk in my little store-room and office, some lilies and subsequently a book—a dingy, brown paper covered volume, issued by Norgate & Co., or some such firm, and having several passages marked with warratah blossoms. I turned to the first of these and found that it was an Agnostic's views of life, wherein he expatiated on the woe and misery arising from ill-assorted marriage unions, and plainly recommended those he called the victims and living sacrifices to old, exploded notions of morality, to boldly sever the tie, and seek out those for whom they felt they had a real affinity, and there was much more in the same style. The passage was marked in faint pencil strokes and evidently meant for me. I felt hot and cold at once. Evidently Elizabeth —I preferred to think of her by her assumed name—was persistent, and, I feared, in earnest. I took up a blue pencil I used in my accounts, and wrote over the whole page "A Damnable Doctrine," and closed the book, leaving it exactly where I had found it. Some hours after, when I went in again the volume was gone. On the same evening, Elizabeth, I noticed, when waiting on us at supper, gave me one swift, steady look; I avoided meeting her eyes as much as practicable, and the look struck me as defiant.

That night, long after Maggie had fallen into her usual deep sleep, I spent some hours in reviewing the situation. What I wanted was to put an end to all this without a scene (I hated "scenes"), scandal or any disclosures of the past, of which I was nervously fearful. I now believe firmly that through unhealthy brooding over the troubles, real and imaginary, that had sprung from Elizabeth's resolute pursuit of me, I had to a great extent gone off my head. I do not wholly wonder at this, for the trial had come at a season when long delayed and long expected good fortune was at last fluttering her brightest wings full in my mental eyes. A golden future was ahead; a few more efforts and I, too, might take my place among the band of successful colonists, and just at that eleventh hour to be faced by such a trouble as mine, so small and yet so great, so ridiculous from one viewpoint, and so tragic from another, was too much for my brain. I dared not confide in my wife; I had noticed much in her I thought strange for some time previously. I knew well how intensely jealous she was in disposition, and I dreaded to acquaint her with facts which she would, I fancy, receive as insults and wrongs unbearable. I dreaded lest she should imagine that I had something worse in reserve than what I could tell her. I remembered, in bitterness and anguish of heart, how she had told me, with flashing eyes and firm-set mouth, referring to a relative, that she could never trust anyone who had once deceived her; and had not I unhappily declared that until I saw and loved her, no woman had ever received caress or endearment from my hands or lips. Oh, God! In the anguish of self-accusation that dreadful night I sprang violently out of bed, and stamped on the floor!

My wife woke up instantly, and very crossly asked me what I was doing, and complained querulously of being roused out of a nice sleep. "I am dull enough by day," she remarked sharply, "and you might at least let me sleep; what has come over you of late? You are as disagreeable as you can be!"

How could I unfold the truth in face of a demeanour like this? I had, I felt, brought all this misery on myself, and must get out of it the best way I could. There was nothing for me to say. I lay down again and remained still and wideawake until dawn, when I rose quietly, dressed, and went out of the miserable, ill-omened house, and wandered far away into my own solitary fields. My wife, to the best of my belief, remained soundly asleep.

IX.—I am Deeper in the Toils.

The quiet of the fields, very different from what is understood by the word in England, rather contrasted with than brought any balm to my fevered mind; and when as the light increased a hundred parrots began screaming, as is their wont, I longed for my gun that I might blaze away some of my mingled wrath, remorse, and fear. I felt that I had undoubtedly done a wrong thing. I ought, of course, to have faced the trouble and defied Elizabeth (I hate using the other name), and by this time all would have been over. I was conscious, too, within myself of a lurking compassion for the girl; for, assuming that she was not the most consummate of artful actresses, she had been drawn to follow me, as the familiar phrase runs, to the end of the world, and most assuredly I could not discern any possible worldly inducement for her conduct. I felt bewildered among conflicting emotions, and could not decide what was best to do. All I could resolve on was under no circumstances to give this mad, unreasonable girl the slightest encouragement, to hold no communion whatever with her, and to await the event. It seemed to me that masterly inactivity was now the best thing for me. If the worst came to the worst, and a "scene" did ensue, why I could then explain all to my wife, and as in reality I was quite innocent in this unfortunate situation, what need I fear?

I returned homewards rather slowly and meditatively, and was overtaken by one of my men, who had some request to make. When I had done with him, he remarked casually, "We shall have a stir up to-morrow, I fancy, and no mistake."

I started, for I was so wrapped up in my own troubles that I took everything to myself of that kind, and enquired more energetically than the occasion warranted, "What?"

"Oh! haven't you heard? There's a mob coming across here away, one of the biggest and wildest, I have been told, ever seen in these parts. I shall be glad when they're gone. There'll be a nice mess at our big ponds."

I must explain here to the non-colonial reader that mobs of cattle, which frequently muster up to a thousand head, are allowed by law to feed during their journeyings on the ground of the settlers that they pass over, only the law enjoins that they make at least six miles a day, unless, indeed, they have calves. These journeyings sometimes extend for immense distances and occupy many months. Once before I had a large and wild mob of cattle over my land, and did not like it at all, the more so as my wife was very frightened and afraid to stir outside the house until the "beasts," as she called them, had all trotted off.

At present, however, this matter did not trouble me. I was thinking of something much more serious, for it had flashed into my mind with a sinister shock that possibly there might be peril of a kind I had not dreamed of in allowing Elizabeth to remain with us. The book she had evidently placed on my desk put some strange, wild thoughts into my head, and I asked myself, with a thrill, was my wife quite safe with such a companion? Previously—I could not deny it—selfish concern for myself had quite blinded me to what now seemed a very common-sense view of the situation, and I felt that I was, indeed, to blame.

How strangely we are baffled in our best resolutions by

circumstances! That day I could not but be struck by the alteration at home. My wife seemed so very nice, contented and cheerful, and, above all, pleased with Elizabeth! The latter, for her part, had put on a most innocent air, as it seemed to me, who saw her with very different eyes, and neither by look or gesture did she in the least indicate that our relations were different from what they appeared to be before others.

And now I may remark that I have avoided attempting any direct description of this strange creature. The fact is, the subject is far too painful and trying for me to attempt a delineation of a form and face associated with such awful reminiscences. I may say this, however, that Elizabeth was tall, and had a pretty, oval face, with a remarkably firm chin, rather full lips, and the most peculiar eyes I have ever seen in any human being. Ordinarily her eyes were sleepy-looking, but there were times, under excitement or emotion, when they seemed to literally blaze with a devilish fire, as though a concentrated fury looked out of each. Very much has been written about women having eyes of a gazelle, and as a boy I naturally remember the ox-eyed Juno of my early classic studies. To me it has always seemed a kind of degradation to compare the human eyes to those of the animal world, for no one who has studied closely the eyes of our dumb friends can have failed to perceive the radical difference that usually exists between their orbs and those of men and women.

I say usually, because exceptions occur, and the eyes of Elizabeth were a remarkable example of this. At rest and when pleased she had, to my thinking—and others have said the same—the exact look in the eyes that we note in those of an animal. There was a total absence of higher intelligence, but the animal look, innocent enough in the beast, had in her a peculiar sensuality which has led me to associate, more or less, the sensuous with the cruel in mankind; and I am, I may at once say, firmly persuaded that extreme sensuality is necessarily closely allied to real cruelty. Any way, these eyes of Elizabeth could be, when she pleased, terrible in passion as in allurement, and I well remember that, as a boy, she exercised a mastering spell over me by her tender looks, which, during our absence from each other, impelled me in those hot-blooded days to pen a thousand fantastic things which now brought a shudder to me at only their bare remembrance. I have often thought that it must be eyes like these that account for not a little of the dreadful things we read of in history, when men, apparently good and morally strong in themselves, have, through falling under the spell of this intense animalism, plunged recklessly into a downward course of vice, crime and ruin.

Had it not been, indeed, for the long interval that had elapsed between my boyish parting with Elizabeth and her advent at my Austral home, and for the fact that I was devoted heart and soul to money-making, and grounded on a solid love for my wife and child, I know not what my fate had been. I shivered as I recalled one dreadful episode of my boy's experience, when this horrible being, for horrible she now seemed to me, tried to induce me to raise a sum of money on my father's credit and to elope and trust to his forgiveness afterwards! I remember how very nearly I fell, as she twined herself close to me, gentle, warm, and caressing, and pleaded with those soft, melting, sensual eyes of hers, that seemed to sap away one's whole moral fibre, and to relax every nerve. To me it is a miracle that I resisted, but I did; and then, when she found it vain, our first quarrel ensued, and she gave me a touch of the tigress which lay latent in her supple form.

All these things as reminiscences would at odd times come crowding into my mind that day, and they filled me with an unspeakable abhorrence of one whom I had come to regard as a reptile. What had been her experience, I wondered, in the interval, and how came she to emigrate? Doubtless I might have drawn some story from her lips, but I resolved to have nothing to do with her again, and when, in the evening, my wife and I were alone, I spoke out with a bluntness that was no doubt startling to one who knew nothing of what was working and seething within me, and said, quite abruptly—

"You must get rid of that girl."

My wife stared. Evidently she hardly understood me by the way in which she replied, "What?"

"Get rid of her!" I repeated in some excitement. "I hate the sight of her. You don't mean to say you *like* her?"

"Most certainly I do. Why, what ever has come over you of late? You are all pepper and mustard. Matthews was telling me this afternoon that you nearly snapped his nose off yesterday! Poor Elizabeth! She has been telling me some of her troubles, and how she came to emigrate. It seems that she was once engaged to a gentleman, she says, in England, but the parents interfered, and then she had a succession of troubles, but someone advised her to emigrate and thus begin a new life; she was ill a long while in Sydney, and spent all her little capital, then my friend heard of her and recommended her. Oh, Andrew! if you knew all the poor girl has gone through you would feel for her, I am sure. She has quite taken me out of myself and done me much good. I am sure that when we are dull and depressed it is a good thing to concern ourselves sympathetically with the trials of others. You'd be twice as happy, Andrew, if you cared for money less and for people more." And my wife laughed out such a merry, light-hearted laugh that I felt my brain almost turning. "What art had this dreadful girl exercised to obtain such an ascendency as this over my wife?" I asked myself in amazement. "My wife, who was so full of common sense and shrewdness!"

X.—A Terrible End.

The next morning it happened that my wife complained of a sick headache, and said she should lie awhile, adding that Elizabeth would attend to her very nicely.

I cannot imagine why, but I woke that day feeling an extreme depression and a great desire not to go abroad. It happened, however, that my personal attention was, I knew, required some few miles, and I resolved to ride over, transact the business, and come straight home. These great distances are the plague of all Australian cultivators and pastoralists, and tend naturally to much separation and consequent isolation among settlers, especially among those who, like ourselves, were a good way out.

Ever since my wife had evinced a liking for and a confidence in Elizabeth my anxiety had been intensified, and my deep distrust of the girl had now increased a hundred-fold.

"I shall be sure and return as soon as possible to-day," I said at leaving; "you will be able to see me coming back by the Sapphire hill, so look out for me in that track about noon."

My wife smiled in spite of the pain she was evidently suffering, and asked me what made me so very anxious to get back to her all at once, and told me that when I got on Mr. Watford's station, where I was going, and had some of his own fine ale, I should forget all about coming back early.

"You'll see," I cried. "There'll be no ale-drinking for me to-day. I shall return and spend a quiet day indoors for once. We have a mob of cattle coming over the ground, and I shall not be sorry to be out of the dust."

The horse was ready, and I went out. At the porch stood Elizabeth. I carefully avoided meeting her eyes and sprang up, and, as I pulled the horse's head round to set off, she came quite close, and said: "This is the last day." I paused, startled naturally by the queer character of the words, and still more by the peculiar deliberate and half-hissing tone in which she uttered them. I looked the interrogation I did not utter, and then she repeated: "This is the last day," and, bursting into laughter, ran into the house. Never had I heard such laughter, and for the moment I had my foot out of the stirrup and was more than half-minded to abandon my expedition, but, somehow, the whole thing seemed too ludicrous. How could I go in and explain such rubbish to my wife? Had I heard the words aright? Elizabeth had said something that sounded like nonsense, and then had laughed and run in. Well, what could be made of that? It seemed in the last degree undignified on my part to stoop to explanation on such a point as this, and I rode off, only resolving fully this time that, cost what it might, on my return I would unfold everything to my wife and get rid of a being whose very presence filled me with an indescribable abhorrence and a nameless fear.

Goaded on with these thoughts I put my horse along, and reached my friends' station in excellent time, and soon transacted my business. It happened that the station belonged to three exceedingly jolly bachelor brothers, all excellent fellows, ranging from about thirty to forty, and they one and all expressed keen disappointment at my refusal to accept their hospitality. No, I must hurry back. I could not possibly sit down to a rubber of whist. I knew well, from former experience, what *that* meant in point of time. I was plied with questions as to what had come over me, and then one of the three rather startled me by remarking: "And how may the fair Lenore be?"

I stared. He saw my surprise was genuine, and, changing his bantering tone, asked: "Can it be, old fellow, that you don't know what your new handmaiden is reported to do at night, or, rather, in the early morning?"

"Do? My handmaiden? You speak in riddles. My wife has set up a sort of 'help' of late, but I never meddle with domestic arrangements. Wool and wheat are quite as much as I can manage." And I laughed rather a forced laugh, for I now felt that the eyes of all three were fixed on me in a very curious manner.

"Well," observed the eldest, "you don't seem to know aught of the matter, and perhaps it is none of our business to tell you. However, you ought to know that your handmaiden is given to an early gallop, Joan of Arc fashion, when she thinks there are none to see her; but she is seen all the same, and she rides in such a daring way that one of our people was silly enough last week to sit up two nights running to see the sight, and according to his account he was uncommonly near ridden over. I wonder you have not found this out long ago. Is she a somnambulist? That is the general idea."

I was, indeed, startled. No; nothing of this had hitherto come to my ears. And no wonder, for my people were but few in number, and I fear of late I had been rather of a driver, and none of them were likely, except by chance, to discover a nocturnal rider. The intelligence made me very uneasy indeed. What kind of a being was this woman? During my boy attachment I had never noticed anything unusual, except, as I have already said, that she could exercise a species of strong animal magnetic attraction to or influence on others. At least I had felt the power of it; but for the night ride, if truly described, I could not in the least account.

This was a new phase. It quite threw me off my mental balance. What had I done, I asked myself, with a cold thrill of vague but intense fear, to allow such a woman as this to be in our house and about my wife? Anyway it should be ended one way or the other now. I hastily bade my friends farewell, and rode straight home, full of gloomy forebodings and many sharp pricks of a fully aroused conscience.

I had not gone far before I noticed, as I rose on a tolerably high hill, a peculiar appearance in the distance; and familiar with such signs, it struck me that very probably there was a bush fire in that direction.

There had been that season several fires of no great importance, and in my present frame of mind such an incident vaguely spelled out by a peculiar look in the far horizon scarcely affected me at all. I was impatient to be home. Home again; and then—well, then I meant to cut the Gordian knot some way. I could not exactly tell how, but cut it I would!

Nearer and nearer yet. I had entered the last of the gullies and was proceeding at a smart trot, when, just at a bend, where the track narrowed and the great ferns met overhead, forming a natural arch with their beautiful fronds, I just pulled up in time to avoid actual contact with a horse standing still—one of my own, I saw that at a glance; and seated thereon, but not in Maid of Orleans fashion, was Elizabeth Carter! Her face was shaded by a very wide-brimmed hat, and in the twilight of the kind of sylvan tunnel wherein we faced each other I could not distinguish her features very distinctly. The meeting greatly startled me and I said inwardly, "What now move is this?" She on her part appeared perfectly composed. She backed her horse about a yard or so and then managed to completely block the track by turning him half across the narrow way, at the same time extending an arm with a gesture that plainly said, stay where you are. With Elizabeth face to face, I lost my more pressing apprehension for the moment, and, I know not why, a great curiosity as to what she meant and what she really was now seemed to absorb every other feeling. Remember that in my haste that dreadful day I had taken scarcely anything to eat, and a good part of my ride had been under a semi-tropical sun, which had rendered me somewhat dizzy in the head, a fact that I became more and more aware of now I was quietly stopping after my furious ride to and from my friends' station.

"You seem dumb enough now," were the first words that reached my ears; they were spoken in a mocking tone that somehow struck a strange chill to my blood.

"I have told you, once for all, that I will have no kind of communication with you again. Let me pass by. I don't know what has possessed you to ride my horses about like this. If you take my advice, Elizabeth Carter, you'll just ride away. I give you the horse—go your way and let me go mine!"

I spoke out bravely, and remember well my exact words. In truth every word almost that passed between us on that terrible, fatal day has been in a manner branded into my brain for evermore.

"You give me the horse? I am to go my own way Do you remember, Andrew Chambers, what you swore?

Do you remember what you *wrote*—that you would be true to me, that you would send for me although seas rolled between—that you would be true and tender? Tender— yes, oh, God!" and here she shrieked as one stricken with a mortal pain. I felt my face blanch beneath her awful eyes. I knew, miserable man that I was, that it was even as she had said, and I stood for the moment dumb. Was she veritably mad? "Oh no!" she went on, "I see you are flint—indeed you are the slave to that dull glory of a virtuous wife that you used to spout to me about when you were a lover. A lover! I believed you and your poetry, and see what it has brought me to. But if I cannot make you keep your word—liar and coward that you are—I will punish you—ay, punish you. Your wife shall know the kind of man you are; she shall see your fine verses." And she struck her bosom where I suppose she carried that bundle of my foolish boyish effusions. "I am past all care for myself. I have met you to-day to tell you this—to tell you that I mean to blast your home and ruin you as you have ruined me. See!" The torrent of words, which takes some moments to record, flowed from her in one passionate stream, and before I could make a movement she levelled a pistol (one of my own, as I afterwards found out) point blank at my poor horse, and fired. He sank down, shot in the head, and I had only time to throw myself off to avoid being caught under him as he rolled over. Then she turned her horse's head and urged him up the gully at a gallop. I took it all in at a flash, and, in a spasm of intense horror at the thought of what would happen if such a fiend as this woman had proved herself to be should reach my home first, I dashed after her at the top of my speed.

I noticed that in place of a proper riding habit this horrible woman had wrapped round her a large plaid shawl of my wife's, and as she galloped on, a corner got loose and hampered the horse, causing him to stumble and almost fall. This gave me the advantage and I almost came up with the fugitive, but with great presence of mind she caught up the shawl and soon increased the distance between us, calling back once or twice in a shrill mocking tone some unintelligible words which stung me into redoubled exertions. I was in pretty fair condition, and this portion of the gully, which was not really a proper road but only a very rough, irregular track, very up and down, was so far in my favour, and I managed to keep horse and rider in fair view, although even here I could not gain on this mad woman, who rode in a perfectly reckless manner, and more than once, as I could see, was within an ace of being unseated by the projecting branches of some of the trees that overarched the track. Only those who have been running a losing race, and yet determined to win if it costs them their life, can form an adequate idea of that desperate and horrible chase. My heart was ready to burst and the blood throbbed hammer-like in my temples. Now and then I spurted and gained on the horse and appeared almost to fly over the rough ground, and then I seemed turned to a leaden man, staggering wildly over the broken ground and gasping for breath like a drowning man among the surf of a storm-beaten shore. At last the horse shot clear of the gully and I knew that the chase was hopeless. Still I struggled on to the exit, whence I looked on a vast flat that fell away before me, and then—in my wild excitement no sound had reached my ears—I was aware of a fearful torrent—there is no other way to describe it—of cattle pouring across the slope right in front—a torrent of tossing heads without beginning or end as it seemed.

It was an appalling stampede of cattle, such as I had never seen before, and as I looked the flying horse charged right into the flank of this roaring, bellowing river of terrified, maddened beasts, and disappeared from sight! Then as I looked, hardly comprehending what had happened, the awful tightness that seemed to confine my heaving chest like a biting chain of steel relaxed. I lost at once all sense of pain and terror, and, as it appeared to me at the time, sank down, down, deep into the earth that yielded before me as water, and with the sound as of many waters in my ears, I passed into complete oblivion, and for a time was, as it were, annihilated.

There is little more for me to tell. By the most careful and tender nursing my wife brought me through a most perilous illness, and, as the doctor insists, did far more then he to effect a complete recovery. In my intense exertions to overtake the flying horse which had been goaded into a gallop I broke a blood-vessel, and was thus saved very probably from the awful death that befel its rider, whom subsequent evidence proved pretty conclusively to have been both a somnambulist and a monomaniac. My wife's friend who recommended the unhappy girl to us kept back facts that had really come to her knowledge, viz., that on the voyage out Elizabeth Carter had a severe attack of brain fever. My wife knows all.

There is no more any veil between us, and she is, I know, mightily proud of her skill, patience, and tireless attention in "snatching" me, as the doctor put it, "right out of the jaws of death."

We are now happy and prosperous, and our boy is growing up strong, bright, good, and clever. There is no speck on the clear horizon of our life's sky, excepting only that ill-natured and altogether abominable scandal set on foot by my political opponents, who have used the "Carter affair" as an agency for a cruel attack on me personally. It is to meet and crush these foul slanders that I have determined to set forth, as I have done above, the truth, the whole truth, and nothing but the truth.

SKETCHES, &c.

AUSTRALIA TO ENGLAND.

1887.

We warmly greet thee, England's Queen,
    From every Austral land,
United by the seas between,
    Those bulwarks true and grand,
That made us great and keep us free,
And hymn with us thy Jubilee!

It is not yet a hundred years
    Since Sydney first arose,
Unbought by blood, unstained by tears
    Of conquered nations' woes—
Of honourable toil the fee,
She joins with us thy Jubilee!

Thy shield is charged with glories rare,
    We have our triumphs, too,
In clusters here, of Britains fair,
    And, England, all from you!
What wonder is it then that we
Are joyous at this Jubilee?

The victories of Peace we claim
    Beneath the Austral sun;
Our shield hath not one blot of shame,
    Our wealth is labour-won;
And o'er the waves, with Saxon glee,
We greet, oh Queen, thy Jubilee!

From golden Melbourne's stately streets,
    From Adelaide the fair,
From Brisbane with its tropic heats,
    From Auckland's cooler air,
There ringeth forth from Peoples free
The chorus of thy Jubilee.

Australia wears no threatening sword,
    But she can guard her own;
And, England, if a foreign horde
    Assailed the Island Throne,
All Europe—all the world—should see
Australia's one in blood with thee!

EDWARD GIBBON WAKEFIELD;

AND

HIS WORK IN NEW ZEALAND AND AUSTRALIA.

HISTORICALLY England is the one grand exception to the rule that empire has usually been achieved through the concerted action of statesmen, that is, through *government*. In the case of Great Britain the creative political force has been the *individual*, and too often governments have actually opposed, and even frustrated, grand efforts made by far-sighted patriotic men for the development of the national strength and the extension of the national dominion. All the ancient empires were systematically built up on the governmental plan. France, Germany, Russia, and indeed every one of the powers of the Continent, has been reared on a like basis; but with ourselves, owing to *party* being the fundamental principle in the State, no general national concerted action has ever been practicable, and hence what has come to England of imperial greatness has been principally the work of individuals, who have often had to fight against their own government as well as against the natural difficulties in their path.

This, indeed, is one of the main causes for that extraordinary political ingratitude and apathy towards some of our very greatest men so noticeable in English history, and thence it has come about that if it is not exactly true that England knows nothing of her greatest men, it is certain that the mass of the people know comparatively little of some of them.

Happily there is always an historical court of appeal, and I propose here, in as succinct a manner as possible, to rescue one who was in some respects our foremost and most gifted colonial statesman (a statesman, however, outside the precincts of St. Stephen's) from the partial oblivion which has so unjustly descended on his name and concealed from the general public the character and magnitude of his services in founding our Austral colonies.

It is now more than a quarter of a century since there passed away at Wellington, New Zealand, at the age of 66, after a distressing invalid existence of seven years, Edward Gibbon Wakefield, of whom it is not too much to say that he, more than any other man, contributed to consolidate the present Australasian dominions. Yet how little, comparatively speaking, is known of him! In 1876 a subscription was started, headed by the late William Purdy, of the Bank of South Australia, to place a marble bust of Wakefield in the vestibule of the Colonial Office, and a very valuable collection of his letters, relative to the settlement of Canterbury Province, New Zealand, was reviewed favourably some years ago by the *Saturday Review*, but the mass of the people do not greatly heed a bust in the lobby of a Government office, and still less over 300 pages of correspondence whereto they hold not the key.

Let us then briefly sum up some of the salient points in the public life of this remarkable man.

First of all, he is the author of the system of colonisation under which public lands in the colonies came to be sold, in place of being given away, the proceeds being devoted to emigration, surveys, roads, churches, and schools. This was a most important economic reform. Then Wakefield's great book, "A View of the Art of Colonization," is really a standard work, and was so described by John Stuart Mill. But Wakefield was a maker of States rather than of books; he had the special organising and formative mind of the statesman who rises high above the whole region of party—or shall I say professional?—politics; and if we take, first of all, his general services to the cause of emigration, we shall perceive that here alone he wrought, in the teeth of enormous difficulties, a great, an expansive and enduring work. Let us remember that he was the first in the present century to persuade *respectable* persons to emigrate. During the spacious times of Elizabeth, and far later than those, gentlemen had emigrated, but after the declaration of American Independence, a change ensued. The thing wore a new aspect owing to the practice of transportation for such a wide range of crimes, and at the beginning of the present century a respectable retail tradesman considered it a disgraceful thing to have a son who had emigrated. There is no doubt that ignorant people confounded colonists with convicts, and we know that even now something of this old prejudice still lingers, and "colonials" are not unfrequently regarded coldly by certain sections of society. Thus, a shade of scorn has even passed to the honourable order of St. Michael and St. George, because it has been extensively bestowed on distinguished colonists.

Wakefield was unquestionably the first to oppose and overthrow the strong prejudice that existed in his day against emigration in the minds of the respectable, and especially the well-born and upper, classes. As an evidence of his success in this we have only to reckon up the leading men whom he either induced to try their fortunes at the Antipodes, or to take an active part in promoting emigration thither. That men like the Lambtons, the Lyttletons, the Petres, the Molesworths, Tancreds, Dillons, Cliffords, Welds, Hanmers and hosts of others should be won over to colonisation proves that Wakefield must have been as convincing in argument as he was earnest in principle, and alone marks him out conspicuously as a born leader of men.

And then only consider the serious difficulties that in those days stood in the path of the emigrant. Look at the length of the voyage, the absence of telegraphs, the tedious mails, the very different equipment of the ships of those days, the fact that the Maoris of New Zealand were known to be cannibals, and marked besides by an intense ferocity towards all strangers. Then, too, there was the fearful sense of complete isolation, and the entire cutting off of the well-to-do and educated emigrant from all the enjoyments and triumphs of English social existence—a complete abandonment of all that constitutes the pomp and circumstance of life at its best. Surely a man to win over men such as he did, must have had a strange magic in his manner, and that masterful will which belongs, indeed, especially to the founders of States.

It was by Wakefield that, in 1837, an association was formed to colonise New Zealand, an association subsequently known as the New Zealand Company, 1839, and eventually the New Zealand Company, which founded the settlements of Wellington, Nelson, New Plymouth and Wanganui.

At the close of 1843, Wakefield conceived the grand idea of a Church of England settlement in the Britain of the South; and, although difficulties were, as usual, encountered, the project began to take shape two years later. Among those who took a warm interest in the project was Archbishop Whately.

Unhappily here, as has so often happened in our "rough island story," the Government was distinctly against the individual who was seeking to extend the empire; and Earl Grey, who in opposition had been sympathetic with these colonial schemes, when in power yielded to a foolish and prejudiced influence from "Exeter Hall politicians," and sought to destroy the New Zealand Company which Wakefield had created, and from which such enormous Imperial gains were to spring. It is not surprising that the great shaper of the Australasian destinies of England should have yielded at last to the effects of undue brain pressure and disappointment, and he was struck down by serious illness, and for some considerable time was invalided in a cottage at South Stoke, in the delightful valley of the Arun, just under the walls of Arundel Park, Sussex. He then went to Great Malvern to undergo hydropathic treatment, and then became acquainted with Mr. Godley, an acquaintance cemented afterwards into an enduring friendship.

Then came the grand scheme for the settlement of Canterbury, New Zealand, and he almost persuaded Sir William Bellairs, of Mulbarton, near Norwich, to emigrate with his whole family and property—the latter about £70,000. This fell through; but it served to show how great an influence Wakefield exercised in England in regard to emigration.

It was ever a desire of his to spend his closing years in the fair land where he had done so much to reproduce England; but to him it was as a duty to work on at home in the cause of that great colonisation which he had himself created, and he was in fact able to do more here than he could on the other side. In the year 1848 he resided at Boulogne for the special purpose of writing the book referred to above on the art of colonisation, and a work playfully referred to in his correspondence as "My Mrs. Harris," because it had been long projected and friends thought it would never see the light. This work, however, was finished, and when at length the New Zealand Constitution Act was passed, Wakefield felt that his great life work was in a manner accomplished, and in 1853 he arrived at Lyttelton, and had the pleasure of seeing the great settlement he had created. But he was not a man to rest on laurels, however bright.

He embarked on the troubled waters of New Zealand politics, and became a member of the House of Representatives; and, being assailed by his political opponents —he was dead against the delusive cheap land scheme of Sir George Grey—he gave a memorable address of over five hours' duration. Exhausted by his oratory, he returned home against a south-east gale in an open vehicle and fell ill. Unhappily he never recovered, and for seven long years of suffering he endured the martyrdom of a sick chamber, dying in May, 1862.

Such is a feeble and comparatively colourless outline of the work of Edward Gibbon Wakefield. Let us not forget that to him we owe not simply the colonisation, but the very possession of New Zealand. Had not Wakefield by his daring but quite irregular act of sending out an expedition to colonise New Zealand, without— observe—waiting for *Government* sanction, the Government of the day would not have been in a manner forced to take possession of the Britain of the South. There is no doubt whatever that France would have seized New Zealand. It is well known that England took actual possession of the Southern island only a few days before the French ships, commissioned for the same purpose, actually arrived off the coast!

Rarely has there been in history such a race between two rivals, and here, as we see, the individual completely triumphed over the Government. Obviously Australia owes an enduring debt of gratitude to the man whose energy, courage, and forethought preserved New Zealand from being occupied like New Caledonia. Think from how many perils Australia has been preserved; for if New

Caledonia is a thorn in the side of the Austral Dominion, what would a French New Zealand have been? Then, as far as Australia is concerned, let it be never forgotten that Wakefield was the principal founder of Adelaide.

Let it be remembered that he not only practically founded the cities of Wellington and Nelson, but he founded also Christchurch and Dunedin, for the late J. R. Godley and Captain Cargill were his lieutenants, so to speak. Will it be credited by the general reader that in none of these cities is there a statue or public memorial to his honour? Christchurch alone has a fine portrait of him, by Collins, R.A., but even that was presented by *English* subscribers.

At home there is, indeed, the bust in the vestibule of the Colonial Office, whereto I have already referred, which bears the subjoined inscription:—

"Edward Gibbon Wakefield, author of the 'Art of Colonisation.' Born in London 20 March, 1796; died in Wellington, New Zealand, 16 May, 1862. To commemorate his statesmanlike qualities and his disinterested efforts for the improvement of the Empire, his friends and subscribers have presented this bust to the Colonial Office."

Some reference ought in justice to be made here to Wakefield's brothers. Captain Arthur Wakefield, R.N., after very long and distinguished service in the Royal Navy, sailed for New Zealand, and founded the colony of Nelson in 1841. Captain Arthur belonged to the type of Drake. He was under fire, and a heavy one, too, at Batavia, when only 11 years old, and actually captured a standard at Bladensburg when but 14!

At Nelson he did very much service to the new-born colony, and was deservedly popular. Unfortunately he was killed during the lamentable massacre of Wairan on June 17, 1843. He had surrendered to the rebels, but was murdered in cold blood by the scoundrel Rangihaiata, who, to the shame of the colony, was shortly after fêted and caressed by the Governor and Bishop of the colony. The death of Captain Arthur, and that of those who fell with him, were never avenged, and the colony of Nelson seems never to have recovered from the untimely death of Captain Arthur Wakefield.

Then Colonel William Wakefield, after greatly distinguishing himself in the constitutional cause in Spain under Sir De Lacy Evans, led the first body of English colonists to New Zealand and founded the city of Wellington in 1839. He first arrived in Port Nicholson on September 20, and was at once struck by the magnificence of the nature-made harbour and by the central character of the situation. There was much opposition offered by the Governor of the colony, who founded Auckland for the express purpose of thwarting the New Zealand Company, which really was to the colony what the old East India Company was to India, but the wisdom of Colonel Wakefield's choice was finally justified, for Wellington has now long been the capital of the colony. From 1839 Colonel Wakefield conducted the affairs of the Company in the face of the most appalling difficulties and his premature death in 1848 was universally deplored. His funeral was marked by many honours and he was followed to the grave by the Governor, and all the army and navy officers, together with virtually the entire body of settlers. There is, I believe, a fund at Wellington for the purpose of founding some fitting memorial to his memory, but, from one cause or another, it has never yet been applied.

Some passing reference should be made here to Daniel Wakefield, Attorney-General of the Southern Province of New Zealand, and one of the earliest judges of the colony. He was the elder brother of the two already mentioned, and was commissioned by Colonel Wakefield to negotiate the purchase of a great part of the South Island, including the site of the now famous city of Dunedin.

That the Empire, indeed, owed much to the Wakefield family must be obvious, but I must not pass over entirely unnoticed the great Canadian work of E. G. Wakefield, although, of course, this has but a remote bearing on Austral interests. It is surely worthy of record here that the Earl of Durham, Governor-General of Canada during a most critical period, wrote in a book which he presented to E. G. Wakefield that all the successful acts of his government were due, and had been performed by Wakefield's advice, and that all the unsuccessful acts had been when he acted contrary to that advice!

It follows, then, that the Wakefield family—this noble and gifted band of brothers—has really wrought out great things for the Empire, and have emphatic and, indeed, irresistible claims to be remembered as among the foremost of England's best sons.

One word more. Edward Gibbon Wakefield, whether in the persons of his brothers or others, had brave and loyal lieutenants to serve him and carry out his grand and comprehensive plans. His was the creative and formative mind, and theirs the powerful executive. No man ever did greater work with more limited means or in the teeth of such tremendous obstacles. Yet Wakefield lived to surmount and triumph over them all; but he also lived amid galling neglect and misunderstandings, and was ill-recognised by the nation for which he did so much. Probably our annals rarely, if ever, exhibit a man of equal capacity and power who was so little of a self-seeker. What he had—and that was, emphatically, governmental genius—he gave royally for the benefit of his countrymen, and in preserving New Zealand from France, he conferred a benefit on mankind, as a French New Zealand would inevitably mean war in the Austral world.

To write the true history of the founder of New Zealand as a colony, would require at least a volume. Here I have but ventured on a modest monograph, impelled by the fact that on looking around in current Australasian history for some fitting record of this great man, I found it not. It is, therefore, in the interests of biographical truth and historical justice that I adduce the above testimony to the inestimable services of a man to whom England owes, indeed, much, and Australia and New Zealand infinitely more.

TASMANIA:

A SKETCH AND A PROPHECY.

Some time since a Chicago journal boasted that within a few years the neighbourhood would swarm with a population of full five millions! This seems to me, *per se*, by no means a matter for national trumpet-blowing—unless, indeed, we could know that the *quality* of these citizens to be would at least bear some proportion to their numbers. I often fear that some of our Australasian pioneers are inspired by the same fatal craze for numbers and size, forgetting that, after all, in human, as in all other things, *quality* alone will bear the test of time and the vicissitudes of fortune.

Athens was a small city, and the Athenians were capable of being all stowed on board two or three of the P. and O. steamers—that is, the leading citizens; yet they live to us, while millions and millions of the "barbarians" around them perished utterly, and left no sign behind.

Thus, it may be positive gain to a community to want unlimited "elbow room," and to find itself within natural conditions which operate as a matrice to condense and give definite expression to the natural bent of its national genius.

Bigness is all very well, but it has necessarily nothing to do with greatness, although this is frequently overlooked.

Comparatively speaking, I judge that Tasmania is, of all members of the Austral group, the least known to average non-colonial Englishmen and women, which is, in truth, a strangely ironical paradox, seeing that it is a far more perfect analogue of Great Britain than New Zealand, and that in a far greater number of physical circumstances it recalls to all natives of the United Kingdom who once visit it the best and most endearing features of England, especially England as she is embalmed in the cameo-like sonnets of Wordsworth or the sweet and pure domestic lyrics of Mrs. Hemans.

It has sometimes struck me that Tasmania is just a little like the formation that might be anticipated if Titans, like those the ancients fabled, broke off a roughly heart-shaped portion, about the size of Ireland, say, and managed to preserve the loveliest of our lakes, the most picturesque of our Welsh mountains and Devonian hills, the most delightful of our rivers, the fairest of our typical valleys, and the healthiest of our table lands. Yet even this would be far from all that Nature herself *has* done for the real Tasmania of the Austral world, since there we have forests, vast and dense as those which marked England in the Feudal period, when the oak was a power of the land, and over fifty islands clustering about its shores; while its sinuous coasts exactly resemble those of the British Isles in the number and magnitude of the nature-made ports and harbours that have been so freely provided.

Physically we have here an analogue of a highly condensed England, blessed, as many have declared, with the climate of Italy, minus some of the drawbacks there, for Tasmania has summers devoid of scorching heat, and winters that bring cheery and bracing frosts and sunshine almost always bright.

Few, I believe no, countries of the world are so well watered with rivers, many of which arise in the table lands from natural reservoirs of some of the best water in the whole world. The Derwent, the Tamer, the Mersey, the Esk, North and South, and many others spread fertility and beauty throughout the interior, while of the lakes, that known as "the Great" covers an area of 28,000 acres, and Lake Sorell, in Westmoreland county, extends to 17,000 acres.

The climate has been compared to Cheltenham during summer and to Sicily in winter, and some say that in that season it resembles Lisbon. Any way it is free from keen and nipping cold east winds, damp fogs and all the thousand and one malign influences which so frequently convert the English climate into *weather* simply, and weather that is invariably bad.

No other part of the Austral world furnishes such a low death rate for infants, and *that* is conclusive testimony to the vivifying qualities of the air and general meteorological conditions. The usual death-rate is but a decimal point or two over 16 per 1,000, and the ordinary "cause" of death to residents in this nature-favoured colony, is just that one really incurable disease—old age.

Whether we take seascape or landscape, the prevailing appearance of still life is thoroughly English, but it is English in a highly concentrated state, as though all the commonplace, monotonous dead-levels had been, by some violent but æsthetic spasm, squeezed up into a pocket Lake District, a pocket Wales and a fair reproduction of Devonshire and Somersetshire, with a few more of our most picturesque counties thrown in.

The greatest and most charming varieties of scenery are common sights in Tasmania, where we have within the range of one eye-sweep of the horizon the snow-crowned mountain peak, the crystal lake, the green valley, the undulating pasturage, and the well-tilled fields, such as form the pride of agricultural England. This is not all. Garden, and hedgerow, and well-kept road exactly recall to mind rural England, and the new arrival cannot without difficulty forget that he has left the land which he finds so wonderfully reproduced by nature and industry beneath the Southern Cross.

Although there are now no noxious animals, the fauna is numerous and includes over 150 birds, among which are larks, magpies, blue wrens, sandpipers, gulls, teal, duck, herons, bitterns, and very many more, to say nothing of swans and cockatoos.

The rivers and adjacent seas are well supplied with fish, and salmon, salmon-trout, and trout have been acclimatised. The local flounder, rock cod and trumpeter compare most favourably with salmon or turbot.

The flora includes quite a thousand indigenous plants,

and flowers dear and familiar to English eyes bloom prolifically.

The forests are veritable mines of wealth in timbers, many of which, like the well-known Huon pine, the red myrtle, and various species of gums, are of undoubted value and thoroughly merchantable, whenever proper trade openings shall be provided for their outlet.

The mineral wealth of Tasmania is at present but imperfectly known. The marvellous mountain of tin—Bischoff—is but a type of other like deposits, and besides silver, lead and gold, which undoubtedly exist in great quantities, we have on the east coast a vast region where iron and coal can be worked in enormous quantities.

At present the smallness of population has effectually kept Tasmania in the rear, although of late the fine fruit put on the London market by Tasmanian growers has attracted a little attention to the island colony. Unlike some other sections of the Austral dominion, Tasmania has been spared any great social throes. It is not by any means, socially, a land of millionaires, but it is the land, *per se*, of comfortable competence, of domestic enjoyment, of true social solidity, and has less want and suffering, less vice and crime than any other corner of the whole British dominions. Here, in truth, where a Cabinet Minister receives but £900 a year, we have a community really keeping the golden mean; and here, curiously enough, where the inequalities are the least, and the middle class prosperity of England seems to flourish best, we have that intense loyalty to the old country and to the great principle of federation, whereon alone the future Austral Empire can be securely founded.

It is, then, no wonder when Tasmania sees herself a fairer England, an ideal country beautifully planned out by a benign Nature, and so far aided by fortune into the attainment of a flattering miniature of England, such as Sir Philip Sydney loved and died for.

All this happy social state has come about naturally enough. The results speak eloquently for the moral quality and pith of the pioneers of the colony; but much might now be done beyond if some sort of general direction were now given to what seems to me to be the genius of the colony. ·I know well that the Anglo-Saxon has a distrust of Governments as shaping powers, and while he has utter faith in himself individually, he feels grave doubts when he has to be dealt with collectively. Yet it is certain we should gain enormously by making what use can be wisely made of the formative hand of Government, and by sometimes forming a well-matured matrix of future human usefulness, wherein population may be gradually poured, so as to work out double results simultaneously, viz., prosperity for both the individual and the community. And be it noted by those who cavil about "paternal rule," that the gain to the community ultimately benefits the individual, and is to him or her, in point of fact, a pure gift.

The population of Tasmania is about 150,000. Of these, say, 75,000 are males, and then, if we deduct thence the very young and the old, we shall not have above, in round numbers, say, 25,000 men to account for the present material prosperity of the colony. Truly, this community, which reminds one much of one of the ancient confederate Greek States, has accomplished not a little. There are, to begin with, nearly half a million acres of good land under cultivation, whereof on March 31, 1887, 40,498 acres were under wheat, oats 21,169 acres, and potatoes 42,526. Then 793,130 acres were leased from the Crown chiefly for pastoral purposes.

For 1888 the sheep were reckoned at 1,547,242, the cattle at 147,092, the horses 29,528, and the pigs at 52,508. The wheat yield is high and good, and the fruit harvest is simply abundant and overflowing. Jams and green fruit to the value of £139,901 were exported in 1887. The railways extended 318 miles, and the telegraphs 2,407 miles.

The public revenue for the year 1887-88 was £594,976, while the imports were valued at £1,449,371, and the exports at £1,596,817.

This is pretty well for less than twenty-five thousand men as a working force.

If, however, we turn to shipping, we shall find here the same marvellous progress. On December 31, 1887, the total registered shipping was 34 steamers and 174 vessels, with a tonnage of 16,948. The inward entries were 677 (tonnage 360,404), and the outward entries were 714 (tonnage 348,773).

Evidently there is great activity in the mercantile marine of the island colony. The future of Tasmania seems greatly to point towards maritime enterprise such as has not yet engaged any member of the Austral group.

When Mr. Firth, of Auckland, lately visited the United States, he specially noticed the utter decay that is taking place there of any interest in seafaring matters. The people of America are turning their faces inland

and the race of sailors is dying out. In like manner will it be, to a considerable extent, in continental Australia as the railways open up the interior more and more to occupation. But as Tasmania becomes more populated, the drift of industry will be, if I mistake not, rather to than from the sea. The matchless natural harbours which abound everywhere, the many good docks that exist ready made, cannot fail to attract capital and labour. Dredging, of course, is needed, and probably a vast amount of constructive engineer's work; but all this will come, and undoubtedly ore and timber exist in unlimited quantities, and need but to be opened up to present Tasmania in an entirely new aspect to the outside world.

Tasmania is by nature destined to be the maritime member of the Austral group, and she will eventually engross the carrying trade of her sister communities.

Under proper financial organisation and Governmental direction, there is no doubt that Tasmania might be made a great shipbuilding colony; and from her many ports of the future—ports that could easily be made impregnable—might issue some day the dominant navies of the Southern Ocean.

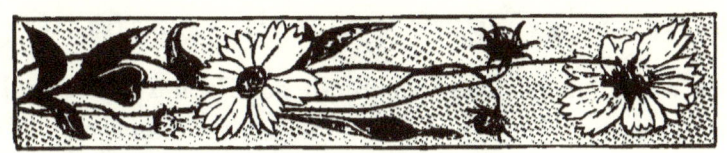

VICTORIA AND ENGLAND:

A CONTRAST AND A SUGGESTION.

VICTORIA—the smallest, in point of area, of the Austral continental colonies, and, as a colony, not yet half a century old—is altogether the most remarkable of all members of the group in regard to material wealth and moral progress. Its entire area comprises 87,884 square miles, and the population is, in round numbers, slightly over a million. The climatic conditions are wonderfully good; there is a birth-rate of 31·23 per 1,000 (1886), and the death-rate then was only 15·15 per 1,000. In round numbers no less than 2,500,000 acres were under successful culture, over 1,700 miles of railways were completed, and the telegraphs extended over 4,094 miles in 1886. The mileage of wire was over 10,000, and in a year two millions of telegrams were received and transmitted. The net income thence was over a million sterling, equivalent to nearly five per cent. on the debenture capital. These are big facts and striking figures, and show what can be done by a small population under really favourable conditions. But much more remains. The material wealth of the colony is amazing. In round numbers there are 10,700,000 sheep, and a wool "clip" running to, say, 120,000,000 lbs. There are 300,000 horses, 1,300,000 cattle, 250,000 pigs and 70,000 goats. There are nearly 10,000 acres under the vine, producing 1,003,827 gallons of wine, and 3,875 of brandy. The olive and the mulberry thrive. The output of gold since 1851 is estimated at £212,000,000! Some 1,753 miles of railways are complete, and over 300 miles more in course of construction.

Manufactures have advanced, as there are now 2,813 factories and works, whereof 1,409 employ steam power, and about 50,000 persons—the offensive word "hands" ought not to be used in connection with Victorians. The capital invested in these manufactories is reckoned to be fully £10,900,000. Certainly, Victoria, the smallest in area of all the members of the group, stands first in regard to real wealth and progress. The revenue, raised from a population somewhat exceeding one million, is extraordinary, and plainly evidences how very high must be the average of even the lowest classes. Thus, as an example, in July, 1888, the Budget was found to present a very remarkable surplus, the amount actually raised being £8,236,000. The expenditure, by the way, amounted to £7,398,000. It is little over fifty years ago (1836) that the city of Melbourne, the capital of Victoria, and virtually the Metropolis of Australasia, consisted of but half-a-dozen huts on the banks of the Yarra!

Let us turn to trade. In 1886 the value of the total

imports amounted to £18,530,575, of which amount £8,851,801 came from the United Kingdom. For the same year the value of the total exports amounted to £11,795,321, of which sum £6,566,118 went to the United Kingdom. Then during the same year (1886) 4,631 vessels, of an aggregate tonnage of 3,735,367, and carrying 147,857 men, entered and cleared at Victorian ports. This is but the barest statistical skeleton of the solid prosperity of the Victorian million, and does not include the industrial quickening effect of the mighty sum of gold raised in the colony since 1851, amounting to—if reckoned at only £4 the ounce—£217,572,000, an unthinkable sum of wealth. Nowhere else, I suppose, in the world have the actual and producing industrial forces of such a numerically small community yielded such stupendous results, and distributed among *all* grades of society such a high *general* average of well-assured prosperity. Nor should it be forgotten that the colony contains numberless really admirable institutions of various kinds for mental, moral and religious improvement, and especially for thrift. There are museums, libraries, savings banks, numerous provident organisations, and a host of *bonâ-fide* working men freeholders constitute in this colony the most remarkable and glorious triumph yet achieved by labour, pure and simple. There religion flourishes, and the 200,000 Roman Catholics, outside the ordinary Protestant churches, form a decided contrast to the laxity of religious opinion which unfortunately prevails in other quarters, where indifferentism is helping on amain the subtle and pernicious sap of various immoral free thought movements.

And all this marvellous progress and prosperity has resulted, as we know, from a Protectionist *régime* such as is the opprobrium of the Manchester School in this country. Surely, then, no common interest attaches to an enquiry as to how such a state of affairs has been brought about. The late Melbourne Exhibition alone was enough to impress the whole world with a due sense of the solid greatness of the colony; and obviously the state of Victoria—rich, self-sustained, progressive, and popularly cultured—is a tremendous antithesis (allowing for the difference in point of population) to that of the United Kingdom, now dependent on imports for much more than half the very bread of the people.

I venture to assert that in England the producing class, so far as food is concerned, is approaching virtual extinction. Yet it is certain that the constant increase in the non-producers must necessarily throw the entire weight of the State on external trade props, which clearly may be cut by war at any moment. It is certain, however enamoured individuals may be of the supposed advantage of receiving staple food from foreign sources, that *agriculture*, pure and simple, must after all be the base and core of the world's very life; and it logically follows that the people who voluntarily give the work of their victualling into exclusively foreign hands, must forfeit all true political independence, and consent to live as those who supply their daily bread dictate. To this it really comes in the end, however slow and complex the process be. The outlook, too, is aggravated for the United Kingdom, owing to the known fact that Europe generally scarcely produces sufficient food for the existing population, and thence, if in this country the existing condition of political economy remains intact, the immediate future may see what will, I believe, be at last the inevitable sequel of cheap food from abroad, viz., ultimate famine prices whenever the true pinch shall come.

Now, in Victoria the existing state of things is exactly the reverse. The colony rests securely on the solid basis of a vast majority who are all on a plane of permanent prosperity and of great domestic comfort. Here, then, is the contrast between Free Trade and Protection, and in this case facts are worth much argument. Before saying more of Victoria, however, let us enquire into the true nature of *national* wealth. Whatever enables man to feed, clothe, and shelter himself and family is *positive* wealth. Now, when a man is required to estimate the value of all he has, he naturally reckons the amount of exertion involved in others to obtain like advantages, and that amount really measures his *comparative* wealth. But as *positive* wealth increases, it is evident that *relative* wealth decreases. It may appear Utopian, but if men really obeyed the physical laws that govern creation, each individual (supposing no interference from the greed of others) would possess a full measure of *positive* wealth, and thence comparative wealth would hardly exist. The diminution of *values* would be exactly proportioned to the development and more general distribution of *utilities*. Evidently the value of any commodity is simply the measure of the existing obstacles to its attainments, and consequently *utility* increases as *value* decreases.

Divide a country into thousands and ten thousands of

small holdings and production is immediately developed in the highest possible degree; loss by unnecessarily distant transits is minimised, and the swarm of carriers and non-producing agents is proportionately diminished. Ten farms of one hundred acres each, assuming equally good work upon each, will always yield very much more than ten times the gross outturn of one colossal holding of a thousand acres. And similarly ten farms of ten acres each will produce more than one of one hundred acres. As to the question of machinery, now almost indispensable in many operations of the husbandman in the case of small holdings, it would only be necessary to have them properly apportioned to districts, and hired out as required by the small holders. All cultivation on a small scale when it is on *free*hold soil is remarkable for the quantity and quality of the outturn. This is strikingly shown in the peasant proprietorships of the Continent. Here, then, we have the happy results, supposing the greater part of the soil to be sub-divided into moderate sized holdings, of a greatly enhanced yield of all the necessaries of life, and, at the same time, an enormous increase in the number of actual producers, while the non-producing classes would be proportionately diminished. This, indeed, is one of the most cogent arguments in favour of small holdings, and an argument that must eventually prevail in a country so thickly populated as England. We want most of all to increase our rural population by the magical stimulus of making them freeholders, and by so much to lessen our merely manufacturing population. The great end of the new polity of these islands should be to encourage the creation of *real* wealth and to discourage the growth of *artificial* wealth. People being born into the world must live, and if too great a proportion of a nation have nothing but *wages* to subsist upon, the outcome must be increasing pauperism, social vice, and, in the issue, violent revolution, when emigration ceases to be an adequate social safety valve.

It is certain that mankind cannot live upon wages, but on what wages *produce*. Now if, by a mistaken policy, the wages-earning classes of any people increase beyond a certain ratio to the rest of the population, the period must come when wages will fail, and then they have nothing! This is no extreme assertion; England is tending fast to this perilous point. The safety of any society is to be measured by the proportion of its members who have *positive* wealth, and unless the percentage of this conservative section of the community remains *high*, there is always danger of a social collapse. No revolution dangerous to society can ever occur in any nation where the number of persons having *small* independencies is *great*. The only true independency is that conferred by the possession of *land*, and it is only by in some way creating a large number of small landholders that a fearful revolution in the United Kingdom can be rendered absolutely impossible.

Obviously Victoria is, as we have seen, a most striking contrast to the Great Britain of Free Trade principles, and it is naturally most interesting to enquire into the agencies whereby the great and happy change was effected which, by making Victoria Protectionist, lifted her at once to a place among the communities of the

English-speaking world, which before must have appeared unattainable.

Much of this benign work is that of one man, Sir Graham Berry, the present Agent-General for Victoria, whose political life and services are about co-extensive with the whole effective period of Victorian progress since the separation from New South Wales.

It is but fact to say that Sir Graham is a kind of living chronicle of Victorian history in connection with the marvellous progress achieved during the past thirty years, during which he was engaged in shaping the rough-hewn ends of Victorian life into its present forms of prosperity and power.

In an interview I had with Sir Graham on the subject of Victorian progress, he gave me a sketch of the history of the colony, and interested me greatly by his graphic account of the Gold Field discoveries, which brought in population at the rate of 2,000 a week.

Subsequently there came a time when vast numbers of men, disappointed and heart sick by repeated failure to find gold, crowded off to the capital of the colony, and sought for work at the various trades to which they had been trained in the old country. But here came in a grave difficulty. A Free Trade policy had loaded the warehouses, and encumbered the wharves with a superabundance of the very articles these men were accustomed to make, and as a natural consequence they were soon seen parading the streets of Melbourne in a state of absolute distress.

Obviously the proper and natural outlet for this industrial army was the land. In Victoria, however, a strange state of things existed, and the land was practically closed to these distressed and despairing men, for about seven hundred squatters occupied virtually the entire territory. Reform in the land laws ultimately ensued; but the problem to be solved, was how to deal temporarily with the great industrial problem, so as to retain all this "bone and sinew" for the good of the colony.

It was soon shown that gold, *i.e.* money, is not wealth in a vital sense, and Sir Graham confessed that it was a pitiable time for those who actually witnessed the industrial misery of the day. Skilled mechanics and tradesmen were driven to stone-breaking, and then it was that Mr. Berry considered it high time to form the now famous and historic Protection League, the object of which was to secure a tariff behind which manufactories, mills and workshops could be successfully established.

So indoctrinated with the principles, and, it may be added, the fallacies of Free Trade, was the multitude of the middle and upper classes, fresh from the struggle of the Anti-Corn Law League, that a shout of derision at first welcomed the new movement.

But is it not ever thus with all truly great popular reformers? Agitation and discussion, however, told in time, and branch leagues were formed on the Gold Fields, and at other industrial centres. The Protectionists soon made their influence felt at elections, and in 1870 the Government was defeated on a purely fiscal question, and Mr. Berry then became the Treasurer, and at once introduced and triumphantly carried the famous 20 per cent. duties, which, with some few subsequent modifications, form the basis of the present tariff.

There is no need, in point of fact, to do more than cast a bird's-eye glance over the length and breadth of the colony. There we see, indeed, the monuments of the industrial, commercial, and financial greatness that have grown out of the daring insight which converted the gold-digging population into a nation of productive and prosperous citizens, in what is perhaps the most self-contained, and, all things considered, the most self-supporting community in the world. Nowhere in the world have there been, as there now are in Victoria, such great facilities for the acquisition of property in land and houses by the laborious classes, and thus the whole community is sound to the core, and in the comparative independence of the actually producing classes we have the assurance for a perfectly settled political State—so rarely found in European history. This, and much more that need not be particularised here, would certainly have never been but for the foresight and courage of Sir Graham Berry, of whom it may be aptly said that he knew the occasion when to make the bounds of rational freedom wider yet.

A little fact is worth much argument, and when one calmly reflects on all that Protection has wrought for Victoria, one cannot help seeing how it renders a people, and necessarily so, self-supporting and really independent of all external aid, and capable, indeed, of resisting those external assaults which are ultimately fatal to nations who look in whole or part to foreign sources for the daily bread of the masses.

AUSTRALIAN ART.

AUSTRALIAN Art—some, perhaps, will ask is there such a thing at all? And certainly, to those with only conventional ideas on the subject, it must sound strange to speak of the fine arts at the Antipodes, where gold, wool, and mutton are the great commercial potentates, and the racecourse the great outlet for the recreative genius of the people. Yet if we enquire a little we shall find that, just as there is a growing Australian Literature, of which many evidences have now been given, so there is an Australian Art—a school of Antipodean painters—who will assuredly make their permanent mark in the records of nineteenth century painting.

In reality this Australian art is British to a great extent, as its leading exponents are rarely colonial born, with some notable exceptions, and the Anglo-Australian artist has, as it were, refreshed and revivified his genius by bathing his perceptive faculties in new worlds of loveliness unmatched by any portion of the accessible universe.

In Australia and New Zealand the conditions of life are unique. Many of the settlements have as yet lasted but the space of a single ordinary human existence, and the environment, unlike that of the American people for example, does not suggest aught of history, or even tradition, that might colour or influence the artist. At present no Australian in his own region gazes on a building that is over a century old, and the vast continent has not yet acquired the charm of association. We have no historic rivers, no remarkable monuments of faded or utterly vanished glory, no spots canonised by heroism or devotion, and sending, by their name alone, a thrill to the coldest heart—in a word, there is nothing to link the mind closely to the past, or to impress on it the tender touch of reverent sentiment for decay, which in the old world evokes some of the sweetest strains of song, but, on the contrary, so far as the human element is concerned, Australia is the land of the future, the land of promise and of aspiration.

But if from the painters' view-point we have here none of the features which in Europe furnish of themselves a form of ever-enduring art inspiration, there is, under the Southern Cross, a fauna and a flora and a scenery which are equally unique and extraordinary. Singular are the sights and sounds of the Australian "bush," which in England we should call "forests" or "woods," and strange are some of the creatures that inhabit these solitudes. Thus we are told by an Antipodean poet—

>   The eucalyptus blooms are sweet
>   With honey, and the birds all day
>   Sip the clear juices forth; brown-grey,

> A bird-like thing with tiny feet
> Cleaves to the boughs, or with small wings
> Amid the leafy spaces springs,
> And in the moonshine, with shrill cries,
> Flies bat-like where thy white gums rise.

Such is the "flying mouse" of New South Wales. Then we have the bell bird—

> The stillness of the Austral noon
> Is broken by no single sound;
> No lizards even on the ground
> Rustle among dry leaves; no tune
> The lyre bird sings. Yet hush! I hear
> A soft bell tolling silvery clear!
> Low, soft, aerial chimes unknown,
> Save 'mid those silences alone.

In like manner we have the poetic setting of the rock lily—

> That mighty flower towering high,
> With carmine blooms crown'd gloriously,
> A giant amongst flowers it reigns,
> The glory of the Austral plains.

While of the flame tree we are told—

> For miles the Illawarra range
> Runs level with Pacific seas:
> What glory when the morning breeze
> Upon its slopes doth shift and change
> Deep pink and crimson hues, till all
> The leagues-long distance seems a wall
> Of swift, uncurling flames of fire.

Then in New Zealand we have a new form of Alpine scenery, and probably the famous pink terraces, recently shattered by an earthquake and volcanic eruption, were matchless. They have been compared to a mighty cataract—

> Over a hundred steps of marble,
> But all frozen and dumb.

Or

> A cataract carved in Parian stone,
> Or any purer substance known.

And then there are Mounts Cook and Egmont, and the lovely fern glades and the mountainous Kauri pines, the sylvan giants of the Austral world.

But these are the merest hints of the kind of scenery of Australia and New Zealand, while unquestionably in no other part of the world is there such a pure atmosphere.

These landscape beauties were first attempted by Mr. Gilbert, a pastel painter of considerable talent, but desultory nature; afterwards he relinquished Art, became one of the gold commissioners at Mount Alexander, and married the widow of Sir John Byerly. Mr. William Strutt was the next artist. He made great use of the new material by which he was surrounded. His early records of ancient Melbourne and its environs are now collected in album form, and should find a permanent home in the Melbourne Library. They would be more suitably placed there, I venture to think, than in Mr. Strutt's home. Mr. John Pascoe Fawkner (the founder of Melbourne) soon formed his friendship, and commissioned him to paint his portrait, as also to make a sketch of the opening of the first Parliament Melbourne had. This sketch now hangs in the fine Legislative Council Library.

Mr. Strutt visited the gold fields, and did a little digging and delving, adding to his experience of the rough life all were compelled to live in those early days. The artist then went to New Zealand for 18 months, and here for the present I will leave him, giving a critical account of his work later on, now supplying somewhat the order of other artistic arrivals in Victoria. Mr. Conway Hart's name appears. He was a portrait painter solely, and his efforts met with large appreciation. Then came Eugene de Guerrar, an Austrian landscapist, of keen perceptions. His love for detail found ample scope in the splendid fern trees and rugged gullies of the Australian bush. About this time Mr. Bateman, a charming pencil draughtsman, arrived. He was much employed by Judge Barry to illustrate a catalogue of the Public Library with plant ornamental capitals and tailpieces. He made lovely designs of indigenous plants for fabrics; some of the Manchester houses took them up, and his work in this form (textile) was exhibited at the 1862 Great Exhibition. Mr. Bateman had many friends amongst the Australian squatters, and travelled in the bush. On one of these journeys he was thrown out of the dog cart, and so injured that paralysis of the right arm followed. Nothing daunted, he learned to draw just as well with his left. After a time he left for Scotland, where I hope he may be now enjoying life.

Mr. Nicholas Chevalier, a Swiss painter of versatile qualities, achieved position and success. To him, also, I must refer again later on.

Dr. Ludwig Becker, a miniature painter, contributed all kinds of illustrations to literary work, particularly Dr. McCoy's "Natural History." Poor Becker accompanied the fated exploring party to Gulf Carpentaria, and died at Cooper's Creek, at which place he was making many scientific studies.

Charles Summers, a Royal Academy student, winner of the Prize of Rome for Sculpture, was the first sculptor. He came out heated with the gold fever, and did some digging, but found it uncongenial, and soon discovered a field for his ability in his own line. His principal work in Melbourne is the "Burke and Mills" memorial group at the corner of Collins Street. In London from time to time various portrait busts have been exhibited, and won deserved praise. Poor Summers died in Rome a few years back, and leaves behind him a gifted son still resident in Rome, and progressing most favourably. W. Strutt, Chas. Summers, and Nicholas Chevalier, who may be justly termed the pioneers of Australian Art, started the first exhibition of Art ever held in the colony, under the patronage of Sir H. Barkly.

With these early art spirits Robert Dowling's name must be mentioned. He was first in Tasmania, but after in Melbourne, where he won many friends and patrons; but Australia was to him only a temporary home. He came to England and lived here for many years; visited the East, and brought back useful studies, many of which ultimately bore fruit in important pictures. Mr. Dowling had a number of pupils; some have risen to note, and others are on the road; the sudden death, several years ago, of Mr. Robert Dowling, was keenly felt by his many artistic friends, and the world is poorer and colder now he is gone; and a variety of circumstances removed all the others whose names I have referred to from the land of the Golden Fleece. Here, then, let me come to those who, having returned to Europe, hold acknowledged and famous positions.

Mr. Nicholas Chevalier accompanied the Duke of Edinburgh round the world and made at the time many interesting and valuable drawings, besides finding subjects of such unique nature as inspired him for his "Tahiti Girl going to Market," a picture of great charm in the Royal Academy some years gone by.

This artist is, however, primarily a landscapist, and very lately I saw a splendid picture of Mount Cook rising in all its glory over the great Tasman glacier, which was exhibited in the Melbourne Exhibition of 1888.

Artists' homes are always interesting, and that of this painter especially so. Passing through a small tropical garden the drawing-room is reached, and from thence to the studio, where Mr. Chevalier asks you what country you would like to visit, and on your decision brings out his folios of studies, charming mementoes and delicate impressions of the Pacific Isles, or scorching India, or it may be Madeira, where he spends the winters now. The painter has executed some portraits, and many of his architectural scenes are remarkable for their intricate detail and truthful effect.

Mr. William Strutt is known best to fame as the painter of "Black Thursday," a work of wonderful force and of absorbing interest. It relates to a well-known episode in early Victorian annals. A bush fire caused a fearful stampede of cattle, and much loss resulted both of life and property.

Mr. Strutt is a direct descendant of the famous antiquary, Joseph Strutt, who, as an engraver, illustrated the "Pilgrim's Progress" with great success. He was born in 1742, and died in London 1802. He is best known, perhaps, on account of his authoritative works, "The Sports and Pastimes of the People of England," and several other similar books.

Remotely the Strutts, by the way, come from the Swiss hero and patriot, Arnold Winkelreid, whose glorious and triumphant death at the battle of Sempach is the subject of one of Sir Walter Scott's poems.

In Mr. Strutt's home at West Kensington there are many objects of interest, for as an animal painter he has collected various trophies of the chase, and has made a collection of lion studies that are believed to be unique, and which appear to form a visible history of the royal beast in all his phases of action or rest.

To very many Mr. William Strutt is, no doubt, regarded principally as a painter of animals; but he is much more than that, and may worthily be regarded as both a historic and a religious painter. In these days, when for the Royal Academy of 1889 no fewer than 18,000 paintings went in, there is always a great tendency to the more or less serious obscuration of the finer forms of genius. Life assimilates more and more in the mass to the railway type of locomotion, and the art that is the *acting poetry*, as it has been put. The picture when really good is in great danger of eclipse, total and permanent. In 1889 Mr. William Strutt had in his studio two very remarkable pictures, which, although each represented the labours of nearly a decade, had not been exhibited or in any way noticed; such is occasionally the eccentricity of the artistic genius. One of these works depicts the child Samuel reclining in front of the altar in the midst of the various offerings that his parents regularly presented to the high priest. The pose of the child is equally graceful and natural. He muses and fondles a beautiful kid, and at his feet are some exquisitely-painted pigeons, the eyes in particular being life-like, while fruits, including clusters of grapes, doves in baskets, and a fine calf (a specially good specimen of his genius) represent the fauna and flora of the offerings. The altar, with its horns, forms the background, whence a suggestive smoke curls slowly up. The ritual of the Hebrews, the full ceremonial law of sacrifice, is here typified, while in the one human figure, that of the young Samuel, earnest, thoughtful, imaginative, we see in anticipation the coming regal glories, sublime prophecies of the shepherd king, who four years after the death of Samuel ascended the throne of Judah. The composition of this work, which is of considerable size, is full of details, all of which are harmoniously co-ordinated to the central idea of the picture—the Hebrew rite of sacrifice, the offering up to the Creator of the first fruits; while in Samuel himself there is fully expressed the spiritual perception which underlay the visible worship of the ancient Hebrews, and was so strongly expressed in the Divine prohibition as to graven images. The colouring is throughout rich and fine, and the whole painting is one which makes a deep impression on the memory. In strong contrast to this fine and powerful delineation of a striking phase of the old dispensation, is another work—one that has taken several years to paint

—representing Martha, Mary, and the Saviour at the grave of Lazarus. The grouping is admirable, and the light about the head of the Saviour is a wondrous bit of painting. It is light that stands out distinct from, and yet is subtly blended imperceptibly with, the surrounding atmosphere. The faces of Martha and Mary are wonderfully given. In the former we have in expression and pose the full indication of her somewhat material form of feeling; there is the impatience of calamity and the urgent desire to have it at once removed; while in Mary we have a touching representation of the resignation, the faith, and the spiritual devotion of the true believer, who knows that what is *not* seen is more real than the visible. The yearning of the look, the ineffable love that glorifies, the faith which overcomes all things— all these are somehow (I cannot verbally express how) shown in Mary; and this fills the whole picture with a kind of spiritual atmosphere that touches the higher plane of true religious art. All the accessories to this superb work have been carefully studied, as in the palms of victory over sin and death shown on one side, while afar, on the right as you look, are seen the lamenting and, perhaps then, not over confident disciples. There is complete unity in this work, which breathes forth the very intensity of devotional art, and reminds us how very sacred is the vocation of the true artist who has to do with the works of God, and interpret the teaching of Creation to mankind. Indeed, one is inclined to say, in the face of such a painting as this, that to the painter, as to the poet, is given that divine afflatus which elevates art to the highest plane, and justifies the saying that the highest art is the most religious, for we cannot conceive a scoffing Raphael, and thus we reach that incarnation of fancy which is poetry made visible to the eyes and audible to the soul itself.

The details I have given of those men who have lived for years in the Antipodes may be looked upon as sufficient evidence of the amount of ability these colonies have supported and given birth to, in some cases. Mr. C. E. Hern, late of Sydney (but now resident in London), may be classed with the latter. He has lately adapted his artistic feeling to very pretty and acceptable transcripts of London churches. A special show in Bond Street attracted much attention and brought him many commissions. Mr. Hern is very conscientious and careful in his drawing, and paints his subjects straight off from Nature, visiting the scenes (where much thronged) at early morn.

We now come to Mr. E. Wake Cook, pupil of Chevalier, a skilful delineator of landscape—singularly happy in rendering the aerial perspective of vanishing hills; you can sit and dream yourself away when following his masses of trees or lines of distances blending off into the intangible cloudscape. Whether it be at Whitby, Arundel, or looking across the valley of the Thames, Mr. Cook supplies an air of enchantment to his vistas of soft, fading light. I have seen some of his Italian lake drawings, the mountains coming down to the water's edge, casting their reflections into the placid depths, whilst above vapoury clouds brooded over those glorious heights, giving by their thin veil inexpressible beauty and imagination.

These artists and all I shall refer to subsequently belong to a new and flourishing society—"the Anglo-Australian"—constituted for the purpose of holding exhibitions in the colonies of Victoria, Adelaide, and Sydney; and after, to invite the resident Australian painters to an exhibition here. The list of members is long and honourable; several of the Royal Academy magnates are on the roll and it is supported by the leading artists of to-day—Mr. Yeend King, for instance, one of the strongest of our landscape men. All visitors to the Royal Academy in 1889 will call to mind his successes; and primarily that beautiful type of the old English village street, down which a loving couple are walking to church—for it is Sunday—as quaintly told in the not to be forgotten title, "Between a Saturday and Monday." At the Grosvenor the same year was Mr. King's "Miller," flour-crusted, yet leaning over the doorway of his grist-room waiting for a somebody to pass, and with a bouquet for that body—truly admirable in power of painting and colour, in execution unaffected, and masculine in treatment, tender and strong. Here is a canvas destined to teach the artist and try the critic sorely to describe its charms. Mr. W. Bromley is an artist of the same type, with much of the same view of nature, daring great things, and doing them well—his powerful water colours at the Royal Society of British Artists are impressive in their restrained force. Given but the name of Cox and people would rave over them. I love them as much by Bromley, and more, because this artist can compass *various themes* and deal with each adequately. He gives the wild grey sky over a Welsh moorland, he renders the absolute stillness of a moated grange, where trees look down and see themselves below; and he introduces the accent of interest and life just at the right point, as when a moorhen skims the still waters or swims in coquettish manner on its glassy surface.

I must speak of the President of the Anglo-Australian Society of Artists, Mr. W. Ayerst Ingram, a man of great energy and administrative skill. His choice of subject is usually marine, a large picture entitled "Helpless," representing the wreck of a vessel in a terrific sea, with a group of fisher folk in the immediate foreground, has been exhibited at the Antipodes, and is the joint performance of this painter and his figure-painting friend, Mr. T. C. Gotch, well known in Australia, where he has spent considerable time.

Mr. Gotch has executed excellent portraits and delights in *genre* incidents gleaned from our southern villages.

Mr. H. J. Johnstone, also a painter of *genre*, but principally water colours, has a claim upon our attention. He lived in Melbourne many years, and at that time gave most of his energies to landscape art. I have seen wonderfully characteristic pictures of his of the bush with its gum trees—also others with the gnarled and dead stems standing out, bleached skeletons, against the hot sky, very realistically treated—he always introduces the figure element so happily.

Art seems hereditary in the Strutt family, and the son of Mr. William Strutt, Alfred William Strutt, is a painter of much excellent performance, as well as of great promise, seeing that prior to 1889 he had exhibited, with marked success, at the Royal Academy, and that some of his work has been engraved—a very conclusive evidence of popularity.

Mr. M. L. Menpes is, I believe, a Colonial by birth, and is best known for his sometimes serious, oftener capricious etchings, many a Japanese *motif* forming his theme. He visited the land of blossom and parasols several years ago, and brought back a quantity of material.

Mr. A. W. Weedon is most decidedly a remarkable artist; his Sussex hayfield subjects have fully justified a fame created by his Scotch pictures of spates and storms. Mr. Weedon revels and excels in cloudscape; he renders with wondrous facility the filmy *cirri*, and gives what so few do—the immense distances 'twixt series of cloud masses, producing upon the mind that impression of infinity which Ruskin delights to record and finds such glorious allegories in, and yet in the foreground he lets you down gently to some little homely feature of the hayfield, where tired workmen regale themselves, or happy children play hide-and-seek behind the fragrant stacks.

Most people know, or ought to know, Mr. R. W. Allan's name and pictures, for his powerful method, good colour, and astute choice of subjects are ever something to remember. Whether it be a Dutch canal through flat meadows, and the hay craft floating thereon, or old boats by an estuary of the river, or quaint blocks of houses in some Brittany town, it matters not—each transcript is full of power and feeling. Mr. R. W. Allan is vice-president of the Anglo-Australian Society of Artists.

Mr. W. F. Bishop, known best as the "Bishop of

Burnham," has brought out of that district so many important and truly artistic productions, that it were obviously impossible here to mention them specifically. Visitors to the Royal Academy from year to year have been refreshed and charmed with the beauties wrested from Mother Nature in this neighbourhood. Mr. Bishop is most assiduous; often at daybreak—ah, and earlier— you may find him in his hut waiting for the great day king, and watching for his golden flood of light to tip with exultant glory some woodland slope, and gild the silver birches. These moments of gorgeous patronage are, like all Royal visits, short; and, therefore, the artist struggles day by day to catch a memento of them—and very sweetly he does it.

Mr. Huybers is, I believe, an Australian by birth. He paints figure subjects, but I have not the pleasure of knowing his work. The Anglo-Australian Society is strong in such figure painters as Mr. E. Blair Leighton, the artist of "Fame" in Royal Academy, 1889—an old bard with faded laurels sitting in foreground, disconsolate, and a young singer charming a company of people behind; a thoroughly thought-out canvas. Our sympathies are entirely with the dear old harpist and his songs of yesterday.

Mr. H. S. Tuke is a remarkably able and graphic painter of subjects connected with life on sea-shore and ocean wave, its joys, perils and stern realities. "All Hands to the Pumps" is Mr. Tuke's latest and greatest achievement, and I am not at all sure it is not the finest picture in the Academy of 1889, for, taking into consideration the difficulties to be fought and the uncompromising facts, he has won a victory. Mr. T. B. Kennington has chosen the homeless, workless, joyless, hapless, fatherless, and sometimes almost clothesless, as his models, and with these he makes an appeal straight to the heart. With his paint he can beg most patiently and potently. Out with your purses, ye Sybarites; come over and help us; God has made of one blood all nations of men. These are the works to foster—sympathy for the sufferers—and I hope they may prove a very hammer to break the hearts of thoughtless, self-indulgent slumberers. Mr. Kennington has sought for and found a field for his knowledge of form and scope for healthy sentiment. Lastly—because I wish to interest to the end—Mr. Solomon J. Solomon's name and fame have been so much talked about, it is needless to say more than that he is the painter of "Cassandra," "Samson," and "Niobe," and that his portrait of Serjeant Simon in the Royal Academy, 1889, is undoubtedly the grandest man's portrait of the year. Space fails; there are a host of other names as worthy, such as Leslie Thomson, Charlton (the horse painter), Percy Thomas (the figure painter and accomplished etcher), James Whistler (the notorious picker of quarrels with everybody, but wonderful artist of the etching point), and Arnold, Morgan, Wilfrid Ball, F. Bramley, Stanhope Forbes, W. Wilkinson, G. P. Jacomb-Hood, David Law (the beautiful etcher)—ah! and a host of others. This noble list will show, any way, what Australian and Anglo-Australian artists are doing and have done in the way of art.

UNITED EMPIRE.

Very soon after I became somewhat familiar with the practical working of the Australasian agencies here, I thought what a mistake it was not to locate the whole in a building devoted to them exclusively and appealing silently but eloquently to the eyes of the public in the same way as the Admiralty, the Board of Trade, or the India Office. It is probable that the true value of national education through the eyes alone, by the agency of imposing architecture and beautiful and appropriate sculpture, is not yet understood among us. The ancient Greeks knew well the value of what I may venture to call the politically æsthetic; and who can doubt for a moment that the glories of Athens, as fixed in stone, exercised a power in inspiring her veterans to behave as heroes when far away amid the enervating influences of the Orient? Man is compounded strangely of matter as well as of spirit, and a visible symbol of the heroic is often a great stimulus to heroic deeds. A neglected English poet tells us—

> Heroic leaders make heroic bands,
> As stones turn statues in the sculptor's hands;

and I wish that our public spaces and broad thoroughfares had more teachings of history in bronze and marble to counteract the vulgarising influences that meet us everywhere, and which are omnipotent over the lower and uncultured classes.

This, however, must remain among the things to be hoped and, I trust, worked for, and failing a national and an official habitat for the colonising genius of England, I turn with real pleasure to the solid granite front of the Royal Colonial Institute in Northumberland Avenue, which is in very truth a visible presentment of British dominion beyond the seas in more ways than one.

Unity is essentially fundamental to all really enduring forms of empire, and the Institute, now approaching a quarter of a century in age, has decidedly accomplished very much to unify, and thereby consolidate, British Empire.

The Institute was formed as long back as 1868, when a small band of enthusiastic and patriotic gentlemen, who foresaw what the colonies would become, united to furnish a central point, a common pivot, and a focus for the forces of British colonies to rally upon.

Lord Bury was the first President, and the initial Council included not a few men of the time who have now passed away from among us.

For a while the number of members was small, the funds of the Institute were limited, and the influence of the whole organisation was held in little esteem by outsiders. The base of the Institute, however, had been broadly planned on right lines, and year by year it gathered strength; in 1882 the roll of members contained 2,000 names, and the income was over £3,000 per annum. The Prince of Wales was, as he still is, President, and it was perceived fully that at last the British Colonies had a local habitation in the world's metropolis, whence there radiated forth a power, not included in the book of the Constitution, which was nevertheless mighty, and one that increased with every year. The Council became a kind of Colonial Parliament, most conveniently located in the centre of the Empire, and having the advantage of unifying *all* the colonies into one great representation, and thereby imparting to them that solidarity which is essential to power and permanence in all matters political.

The habitat of the Institute is decidedly a structure in all ways worthy of the purposes for which it is designed, and one that will well serve as a visible monument of the solidarity of the great and growing association to which it belongs.

Well might Lord Bury, in his inaugural address, delivered in 1868 at Willis's Rooms, compare the Institute to a tree which, once planted, has only to grow and expand. The "objects" of the Society were then dimly foreseen, but it was hardly understood how important an office it would hold, how mighty a function it would fulfil as a means for building, or rather welding, together the various outlying portions — now called colonies, but more properly provinces — of the British Empire.

At the "coming of age" celebration of the Royal

Colonial Institute on March 13, 1889, a banquet took place at which the Prince of Wales, the President of the Institution, presided, and in his speech of the evening, referring to the colonies, he said: "I always take the deepest interest in their welfare. It is the duty, if it be possible, of all Englishmen, and, above all, of all statesmen, to visit those great colonies, which will prove to them how proud we may be of being Englishmen, and of what the indomitable energy of Englishmen can do." As to the fears that arose at one time in regard to the Imperial Institute clashing with the Colonial Institute, the Prince of Wales himself said when the subject was mentioned by Sir Henry Barkly, "I can confidently, and most emphatically, assure you that nothing in the nature of absorption of the Royal Colonial Institute by the Imperial Institute is involved in the suggested scheme, as appears in some quarters to have been supposed."

For the peace of the world England ought to be omnipotent on every sea, and this state of things, if it be brought about, will result eventually, I believe, through the action of the principal Australian colonies in building up naval forces of their own, and in creating eventually a mercantile marine over the Indian and Pacific oceans. Influences are ofttimes more than forces, or, rather, they are forces concealed for a time; and it is difficult to overestimate what must have been the value to England in its true political solidarity of the Institute during the last twenty years in checking effectively the many insane but strenuous movements which of late years have been so manifest on the part of the ultra-Liberal party towards disintegration.

An empire of peace—a true and united Christendom—would be the natural and glorious fruits of a perfectly consolidated British dominion, wherein the fundamental principle was all for one and one for all. It is to this great end that the Institute has laboured so long, so well and, on the whole, with such marked success.

In truth, an Institute like that which the Council and the officials have laboured so heartily to advance, in conjunction with a host of earnest and patriotic colonists, is probably of far more real benefit to the empire than any number of seats that could well be accorded to colonists, supposing for a moment that the oft-mooted idea of representation of the colonies at St. Stephen's could ever be carried out. The Institute rises above all party considerations; it has no badge expressive of a political clique; it is essentially Imperial and wholly national. Parliament, viewed collectively, is not altogether a pleasing spectacle to the unprejudiced patriot, who sees therein too many signs of the House divided against itself, while, as we all know, it is exceedingly difficult at times to disentangle the national good from the constrictor-like folds of party envy, hatred and all uncharitableness. In our Royal Colonial Institute we have a kind of revived Witena Gemot of the highest character, a Chamber of Freemen convened for the enduring good of Great Britain in its most comprehensive and world-embracing aspect. I believe it is capable of mathematical proof that the stronger and the more world-enveloping becomes the British Empire, the more is the peace and progress of mankind generally guaranteed, and in days like these such an Institute is not simply desirable; it is necessary. Year by year the best sons of England are more and more projected on the limitless area of the great colonies, and in their union with each other for all external ends and with the mother country, we have the pledge of a coming reign of peace and prosperity such as the world has not yet known.

But it must not be forgotten that both this peace and prosperity depend really on obtaining a foundation of irresistible strength to repel and crush all external assault, and the sole secret of this strength lies in the permanent unity of the empire, whereby, as a correlative consequence, the great ocean highways of civilising commerce, British at all their extremities, or subordinate to the strength of Great Britain, will be preserved inviolate under the red ensign of that mercantile marine which has really won an empire greater than Alexander dreamed of, grander than Cæsar organised.

A MELBOURNE TRAGEDY

AND

SOME THOUGHTS ON CAPITAL PUNISHMENT.

ONE day I had an argument with a certain Agent-General for one of the Australian colonies—it does not signify who or which—on the subject of capital punishment, and in the course of our discussion the Agent-General in question mentioned that many years ago when in the parent colony, he visited Darlinghurst Prison, and saw there the notorious bushranger, Gardner. That Gardner was guilty of some cruel murders seems indisputable, and he was regarded by many who could not well be wrong as a very great villain indeed. However, he was not hanged, as many thought he must be, and my informant found him on the industrial side of the well-ordered prison, actually engaged in the pleasing and innocent task of binding music! This, the arch-criminal remarked, he had taught himself, and he added, "I find it a very interesting occupation." I should add that Gardner might have sat for the original of Haidée's piratical papa in "Don Juan," and was

> ... the mildest manner'd man
> That ever scuttled ship or cut a throat;

and to see him thus engaged in the simple and soothing work of binding music formed certainly a strange antithesis to those who knew the terrible antecedents of the ruffian that had been. In due time Gardner was set at liberty. He left Australia, and was lately—and very likely is now—a peaceful and law-abiding hotel keeper somewhere in California.

I chanced, in connection with the respiting of Gardner and his apparent reformation, to express a pretty strong opinion against capital punishment, and this elicited the following, which, though I do not give names, is strictly true. There was in Melbourne, a good many years ago, a man of what my informant tersely called the "tiger" species—as he added, in human shape—who had a stall in the market then, and used to cause much inconvenient obstruction with his empty crates and cases. This went on for some time, and was found to be such a nuisance that strong complaints were made to him, but always without producing any effect. One evil day an official of the place spoke to him—it must be confessed, rather angrily, for which, indeed, there was ample cause—and "the tiger in the shape of a man" went into his stall, caught up his gun, and shot the man dead.

He was, of course, tried for murder, and found guilty, but through the usual reluctance to inflict capital punishment the sentence was changed into one of imprisonment. The murderer was shut up in a cell by himself, and to him there went as a periodic visitor a Wesleyan minister, who used to exhort the convict to repentance, and spent much time in preaching to him about his sins. One day, when the convict and the minister were shut up together, after awhile groans were heard, but, as such were supposed to proceed from the fervour of religious exercises, no heed was taken at the time; but on the cell being visited it was found that the impenitent convict had actually murdered his charitable and sympathetic friend in a barbarous way, with a weapon made out of a bone saved from some meat, and patiently ground down and wrought into a substitute for a knife. Now, said my informant, "Who murdered the minister?" I need hardly say that the miscreant on this occasion was *not* respited, but hanged; and I must confess that this was a strong case for those who believe in the efficacy of capital punishment.

I thought over this particular case much, and, superficially considered, it must seem conclusive to many minds, but, rightly viewed, it fails as an argument. Bentham says that in the infancy of a State, when anyone committed an offence, the question arises, "How shall we prevent these evils?" and the answer most likely to occur to barbarians would be, "Extirpate the offender." This, however, is simply force in its brutal shape, and has no root whatever in morality. The Marquis Beccaria, in his Essay on Capital Punishment, denies the right of the State to deliberately take the life of anyone, and, as is well known, Count Tolstoi holds the same opinion.

It seems to me, however, simply, that the supposed justification of capital punishment rests on *power* instigated by *expediency* and a strong sense of what is convenient, and not at all on right, pure, simple, and abstract, which is the only absolute basis of true law. The advocates of capital punishment cite cases like the lamentable Melbourne tragedy mentioned above, and deduce thence a strong special plea why murderers should themselves be murdered—for *that* is the right way to express the whole thing.

Murder is dreadful, but, ethically viewed, capital punishment is even more dreadful, and thence it has ever proved, and ever will prove, practically useless to prevent the crime for which it is meted out. The shutting up of a murderer to prevent him from exercising his homicidal propensity is different altogether from taking his life. The fallacy in dealing with capital punishment on the part of its advocates appears to arise from the fundamental idea in their minds that life, *per se*, is the most important and precious thing of which we know. This is really a Pagan or anti-Christian notion, for Truth, Right, and many other purely ethical, intangible things— but none the less realities—are infinitely more precious than the individual animal life of man, although *that* was made sacred even in the case of Cain! It MUST be wrong to deliberately take human life, and I could never perceive why the State or any combination of men should be able to do what an individual manifestly may not do. One of the very worst signs of the materialistic and mechanical morality of the times is the scientific attention being paid to modes of putting criminals to death, when public attention ought to be directed to the question, have we any right to execute them at all?

That the whole spirit of Christianity is entirely against capital punishment under any circumstances whatever is obvious enough; but to descend to non-religious grounds, surely life would be held as a still more holy thing if even the life of the murderer were sacred. How infinitely more awful would the crime of murder appear if even murderers could not be executed! Even suicide, whereto so great a tendency now exists, would unquestionably receive a most absolute check if taking human life deliberately under any circumstances was universally regarded as a thing utterly abominable.

To kill the man who kills is, after all, only the bad old plan of employing force for moral ends. Force is the tool of ignorance at the best. Men and women may be *persuaded* into becoming better, but they can never be forced into a better state of feeling. It is, after all, the everlasting rebuke to those who seem to think that the chemist, the physiologist, and the engineer will be the new triune hierarchy of civilisation, that no sort of *material* agencies alone can ever bring about of themselves moral reformation. It is the eternal rebuke of the spirit to mere matter. The things unseen are the real powers over mankind, and must ever be so, although blind and foolish bigots fighting in the cause of materialism would persuade us that the visible and the tangible are not the unrealities, the deceptive appearances, that they are.

All true and enduring triumphs are those of love, gentleness and mercy; these alone can transform human evil into good, a thing force and ferocity can never accomplish. The *triumphant* crusades of Christianity were only those of the martyrs. When the Christian girded on the sword, even though it were what is miscalled the sword of justice, he relinquished half his strength and became earthy, like the agencies on which he weakly and faithlessly relied.

We may be sure that crime is not killed by punishment, but by the enlightening of the mind of evil-doers and by softening their hearts. It is easy to anticipate the sneers and mockery which such an assertion must evoke from many, but had laws been shaped from the first in accordance with humanity, and not from the impulses of selfishness, cruelty and fear, the world would have had no criminal classes in it now, and if crime did exist, it would have come under the head of insanity alone.

A writer in the *Fortnightly Review* remarks: "Out of every hundred committals for murder in England there result about 49 convictions, and of these 49 convicts about 14 on an average are insane. But besides this, there can be little doubt that many have been hanged who were practically not responsible for their actions. In fact, the whole question of moral responsibility is surrounded with so much doubt and difficulty as to furnish one more strong argument against taking an irrevocable step. The tendency of medical science at the present day is more and more to refer moral delinquencies, in part at least, to physical causes, and it may often happen that a convict's reformation is begun by the prison doctor sooner even than by the chaplain."

Then again, it has been pointed out that if the threat

of hanging deters men from crime, surely the threat of burning or a preliminary course of torture would be still more efficacious. Nay, why not hand over the convict to the vivisectors, and thus at one stroke safeguard society, spare dumb animals, and further the advancement of science? The only logical answer that could be given to such a query would be, that we should in the long run lose more than we should gain. That which is seen would be a diminution for the time in the number of murders. That which is not seen would be the slow but certain deterioration and brutalisation of society by the use of such means. And precisely the same reasoning applies to hanging without torture. As Mr. John Bright well said:—"Whenever you hang a man, if you do in the slightest degree deter from crime by the shocking nature of the punishment, I will undertake to say that you by so much—nay, by much more—weaken that other and greater security which arises from the *reverence with which human life is regarded.*"

Nothing hinders the abolition of murder like the maintenance of capital punishment. The enforcement of the rule for private executions was a tacit admission really of the failure of capital punishment, and the only marvel is that after such an admission it could still keep its appalling place amid the laws of a Christian country—if, indeed, a Christian country can now be found in the sense of the old-fashioned times when some yet dreamed of a common Christendom. Finally, let me conclude by quoting Coombe, who declares that when parents beat their children it is to make them behave well by *force.* When a drunken husband strikes his wife it is with the view of improving her by *force*. When a criminal is punished it is with a view of improving the world by *force*. I answer that the world is invariably made *worse* by *force*, and always must be, and the whole effect of punishment as such has been evil. This obviously does not apply in any sense to mere imprisonment, which is quite another thing and comes under a different category altogether. Finally, I would earnestly ask all who are forming opinions on the subject of capital punishment to begin by enquiring, not is it convenient, or expedient, or wise, but is it *right* to put anyone to death? To this ultimately there can be only one answer.

It has been said by some that the Saviour, on one occasion, sanctioned the arming of his disciples. Far too much has been made of the incident; but to defend is very different from attacking, and if in defence the assailant lose his life, this is neither murder nor execution. As to war, there can be no doubt whatever that all *offensive* war is a stupendous crime, and morally wrong. In a word, the taking of human life—the direct result of the first murder recorded in the Bible—which, by the way, was *not* visited by capital punishment—is, to my mind, distinctly wrong.

The following particulars respecting the Royal Colonial Institute are inserted on account of the importance of the subject to Colonists generally:—

THE ROYAL COLONIAL INSTITUTE,

NORTHUMBERLAND AVENUE, LONDON, W.C.

FOUNDED 1868.
INCORPORATED BY ROYAL CHARTER 1862.

MOTTO—"UNITED EMPIRE."

Objects.

"To provide a place of meeting for all Gentlemen connected with the Colonies and British India, and others taking an interest in Colonial and Indian affairs ; to establish a Reading Room and Library, in which recent and authentic intelligence upon Colonial and Indian subjects may be constantly available, and a Museum for the collection and exhibition of Colonial and Indian productions ; to facilitate interchange of experiences amongst persons representing all the Dependencies of Great Britain ; to afford opportunities for the reading of Papers, and for holding Discussions upon Colonial and Indian subjects generally ; and to undertake scientific, literary, and statistical investigations in connection with the British Empire. But no Paper shall be read, or any Discussion be permitted to take place, tending to give to the Institute a party character." (Rule I.)

Membership.

There are two classes of Fellows, Resident and Non-Resident, both elected by the Council on the nomination of two Fellows, one of whom at least must sign on personal knowledge. The former pay an entrance fee of £3, and an annual subscription of £2 ; the latter an entrance fee of £1 1s., and an annual subscription of £1 1s.(which is increased to £2 when temporarily visiting the United Kingdom). Resident Fellows can compound for the annual subscription by the payment of £20, or after five years' annual subscription on payment of £15 ; and Non-Resident Fellows can compound for the *Non-Resident* annual subscription on payment of £10.

Privileges of Fellows whose Subscriptions are not in arrear.

The privileges of Fellows, whose subscriptions are not in arrear, include the use of Rooms, Papers, and Library. All Fellows, whether residing in England or the Colonies, have a report of each Meeting, and the Annual Volume of Proceedings forwarded to them.
To be present at the Evening Meetings, and to introduce one visitor.
To be present at the Annual Conversazione, and to introduce a lady.

The support of all British subjects, whether residing in the United Kingdom or the Colonies—for the Institute is intended for both—is earnestly desired in promoting the great objects of extending knowledge respecting the various portions of the Empire, and in promoting the cause of its permanent unity.
Contributions to the Library and Museum will be thankfully received.

J. S. O'HALLORAN,
Secretary.

GLASS versus TIN.

EDGE'S "LION" ESSENCE OF BEEF
AND OTHER FOOD DELICACIES.

"LION" BRAND.

Convenient and Economical.
Free from all Metallic Taste.   More Palatable.
Absolutely Pure.
It will keep in any Climate.

ESSENCE OF CHICKEN.	INVALID TURTLE SOUP.
\multicolumn{2}{c}{REAL TURTLE SOUP.}	
BEEF TEA JELLY.	STOCK for SOUP, &c., &c.
\multicolumn{2}{c}{Pure Concentrated BEEF TEA. In Skins and in Tins if desired}	
BRITISH LION SAUCE, THE BEST.	BRITISH LION RELISH, NONE BETTER.

To be had of all Chemists and Grocers.

EDGE BROTHERS, Farringdon Road, London, E.C.

GRIMBLE'S
MALT
VINEGAR

IS

SECOND TO NONE

AND

Warranted free from Adulteration.

HIGHEST AWARD

Wherever Exhibited.

{ NEW ZEALAND, 1882.
CALCUTTA, 1883-4.
NEW ORLEANS, 1884-5.
PARIS, 1885.
ADELAIDE, 1887.
MELBOURNE, 1888.

GRIMBLE & CO., Vinegar Brewers,
Cumberland Market, LONDON, Eng.

SODA WATER MACHINERY

For the manufacture of Soda, Seltzer, Potass, and Carrara Waters; also Lemonade, Ginger Beer, Ginger Ale, &c.

Those contemplating the manufacture of Mineral Waters and the Bottling of Beer, Wines, and Cider, should SEND FOR THE ILLUSTRATED CATALOGUE, showing the various machines required, and giving all preliminary information. *It is forwarded free.*

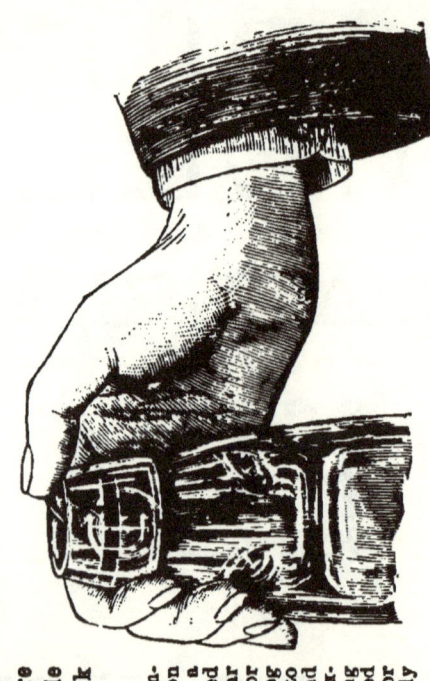

To open, push the wire opener from one side of the bottle neck to other.

By means of this simple but unique invention a child can open a bottle of highly charged soda water without fear of bottle bursting or the contents splashing over. Can be fitted into bottles very rapidly, and makes a permanent fixture of itself and ring also. The "Attached Opener," ready for fixing to bottles already in use.

3s. per gross.

OPENING WITH THE THUMB.

THE GREATEST IMPROVEMENT IN BOTTLES, since Codd's Original, is the

"NIAGARA" BOTTLE,

Which, when fitted with the "Attached Opener," forms

THE MOST PERFECT BOTTLE EVER INTRODUCED.

Those who use patent bottles should see they are fitted with their own opener.

BARNETT & FOSTER, Niagara Works, 25G, Eagle Wharf Rd., LONDON, N.

PRINTERS,

Designers, Chromo-Lithographers,

ACCOUNT BOOK MANUFACTURERS,

WHOLESALE & EXPORT STATIONERS,

179 & 180, UPPER THAMES STREET,

LONDON, E.C.

Colonial Orders receive prompt and careful attention.

PUBLISHERS (to the Trade only) of

SIKES' TABLES FOR THE USE OF THE HYDROMETER.
BATE'S TABLES FOR THE USE OF THE SACCHAROMETER.
SPIRIT STOCK BOOKS, &c.
OWEN'S CONSPECTUS.
SHILLING MANUAL OF PHARMACY.
ELLIOTT & THOMPSON'S COMMERCIAL WEIGHT AND RENT TABLES.

CASH OR LONDON REFERENCE TO ACCOMPANY ALL ORDERS.

www.ingramcontent.com/pod-product-compliance
Lightning Source LLC
Chambersburg PA
CBHW021939240426
43669CB00047B/553